D1275948

The Arapaho Way

Books by Althea Bass

The Arapaho Way
The Story of Tullahassee
The Thankful People
A Cherokee Daughter of Mount Holyoke
Young Inquirer
Cherokee Messenger
Now That the Hawthorn Blossoms

The Arapaho Way

A Memoir
of an Indian Boyhood

by

Althea Bass

Introduction by Frank Waters

Illustrations by Carl Sweezy

Clarkson N. Potter, Inc./Publisher

NEW YORK

For my son, John

COPYRIGHT © 1966, BY ALTHEA BASS
LIBRARY OF CONGRESS CATALOG CARD NUMBER: 66–17885
ALL RIGHTS RESERVED
PRINTED IN THE UNITED STATES OF AMERICA
SECOND PRINTING, SEPTEMBER, 1967

Acknowledgments

I ACKNOWLEDGE WITH GRATITUDE my indebtedness to these people who have helped to make *The Arapaho Way* possible: Mrs. Margaret Blaker, Archivist of the Bureau of American Ethnology, for searching out items connected with the history of the Cheyenne-Arapaho Reservation and the life of Carl Sweezy; Oscar Brousse Jacobson, Professor Emeritus of the University of Oklahoma, for continued interest and advice; Dr. A. M. Gibson, of the University of Oklahoma, for placing archival material at my disposal; Mrs. Jeanne Cook, of the Oklahoma Historical Society Museum, for making possible the inclusion of several Sweezy paintings belonging to the Society; and several friends who lent me their paintings for study or for reproduction here. The photograph of Carl Sweezy and the map of the Agency grounds at Darlington are used courtesy of the Smithsonian Office of Anthropology, Bureau of American Ethnology Collection.

A. B.

NORMAN, OKLAHOMA
JANUARY 31, 1966

74962

CARL SWEEZY

Foreword

FOR SOME YEARS BEFORE HIS DEATH on May 28th, 1953, the Arapaho Indian Carl Sweezy was a familiar figure on the streets of our university town and about its campus. Wearing his broad-brimmed off-white felt hat and his neat, if much worn, clothing, he walked with the rolling gait of the old-time Indian horseman, and he carried a portfolio made of cartons from the grocery store and bound with rope that held the paintings he had come to sell. Few people who saw him realized his importance as a link between the old, free-roaming, buffalo-hunting days of his forebears and the modern Indian who owns his home individually and eats and dresses and makes his living in much the same way as his white neighbors do.

The paintings in his portfolio, too, were a link between the work of the skin painters of pre-Reservation days and that of the modern Indian painters who have studied in art schools and have never lived in a tipi or worn their hair in braids or painted their faces and bodies in preparation for a battle. Born probably in 1881, he knew older men and women who had never grown accustomed to a fixed home on the Reservation to which they had come under the terms of the treaty of Medicine Lodge in 1867, and young people whose only knowledge was of Reservation life. He had seen the authority of old chiefs give way to that of Indian Agents and Army officers; he had known missionaries and teachers and Agency employees who followed the white man's road in everything they did and believed; and many of his contemporaries were growing up in confusion because they could not follow the new road of the white man or the old road of the Indian, and so had lost their way. But Carl Sweezy never lost his way; he saw good along both roads and accepted something of both. The old Arapaho virtues, courtesy and hospitality and loyalty and deep religious feeling, he found to be virtues among the best of the white people too; it was only the methods by which they were practiced that differed. So he could sing Mennonite hymns with the missionaries, and chants with the Sun Dance participants; he could admire the ceremonial dress of some old warrior—headdress, shield, spear, and medicine pouch—and the fine garb of important white visitors at the Agency or at Fort Reno, or later at some gathering on the University campus.

Perhaps it was this two-way course of environment and training that explains Carl Sweezy's achievement as an artist. He took a deep pride in his Indian heritage and always spoke of himself as a full-blood Arapaho. But his associations with certain admirable white people—and he always sought out the most admirable—gave him a perspective, an objective point of view that both intensified his admiration for the Arapaho and their ways and made him see their culture honestly, as something fine and good that was being obliterated. To preserve as an artist what was good and unique and beautiful in a disappearing culture became his purpose, and he accomplished it without any of the embellishments or fusion that might have made his art a hybrid form.

Carl Sweezy knew all the materials and the processes by which the Plains Indians made their clothing, their household equipment, their war and hunting gear. He had sat with old Indian men who straightened willow rods with their teeth and soaked sinews in their mouths; he had watched women dress skins, and sew and bead moccasins; he had played Indian games with his companions and learned to shoot with their miniature bows and arrows. All these things he knew as well as he knew the shape of his own hand.

He was born, like Thoreau, "in the nick of time." Great Arapaho chiefs like Little Raven and Left Hand walked the grounds of the Agency at Darlington and traded at the commissary during his boyhood. He had heard their stories of battles and buffalo hunts and overland marches; he himself remembered the Ghost Dance and Sun Dances and peyote meetings, and Christian religious services of many sects. He never wanted for subject matter; the whole of a vanishing way of life was his to draw from.

Several times Carl Sweezy and I went together to places on the old Reservation that he remembered. At the Agency at Darlington, sadly and dishonorably altered now, he could point out the location of schools and offices and hotel and store; at Concho he knew just where the dogwood used for making bows once grew in abundance. It would grieve him now to know that that fine old landmark, the three-story Mennonite Mission, has been torn down and its site made part of a wheat field. But he never indulged in bitterness. "We had a good time," he would always say, and for him that good time was not lost.

In 1905, in his mid-twenties, on a cross-country tour with an Indian baseball team, he and his companions went to the Lewis and Clark Exposition in Portland, Oregon. He was surprised, and all of them were proud, to come upon some of his work in an Indian exhibit from the Smithsonian Institution. He did not sign his early paintings, and he never kept a record of his sales. But his paintings are to be found in many institutions and private homes throughout the United States, where they speak for the Arapaho.

He never knew prosperity or security. Usually he was hard pressed to buy paper and canvas and paints and brushes, and sometimes, until his later years, he found it hard to sell his paintings. He knew the wrongs that the white man, from high officials to the meanest timber thief from across the Reservation border, had practiced against the Indian, but he never dwelt on these things. He had larger concerns. He was never apologetic about his race or the meagerness of his possessions; wherever he went he walked with dignity among his peers. He never had to make a plea for equality; he was equal. And so, as an artist and as a man, he became a historian and philosopher, though he never thought of himself in such large terms.

The following pages give an account of what Carl Sweezy told me in our frequent visits together. Except to rearrange it by subject matter and to add a few dates, I have not altered it. These are Carl Sweezy's memoirs.

ALTHEA BASS

Contents

Introduction

by
Frank Waters

THIS IS A SHORT, NOSTALGIC, and noble book. It comprises the memoirs of one of the last one-thousand full-blooded Arapaho Indians living on a Reservation in Oklahoma.

When I was a boy in Colorado Springs, a few of them, with small bands of Cheyenne and Ute, still came for annual encampments at the foot of Pike's Peak. I remember their smoke-gray lodges looming against the blue wall of mountains, the smell of their cooking fires, the sound of their drums. The Blue Cloud Arapaho, as we called them, and the Fighting Cheyenne, were the preeminent buffalo hunters, the warrior horsemen of the Great Plains—the fast-riding, war-bonneted Indians who will forever embody the proud myth and sullied history of America.

At the great peace treaty of 1851, made at Fort Laramie, boundaries were established for the major tribes. All the Plains south of the North Platte to the Arkansas River, and east of the Rocky Mountains through Colorado into western Kansas and including parts of Nebraska and Wyoming—a vast domain of more than 122,000 square miles—were allotted to the Arapaho and Cheyenne for as long as the grass should grow; the land north of the Platte was designated for the Sioux, and that south of the Arkansas for the Kiowa and Comanche. The Pike's Peak Rush of 1858, with tens of thousands

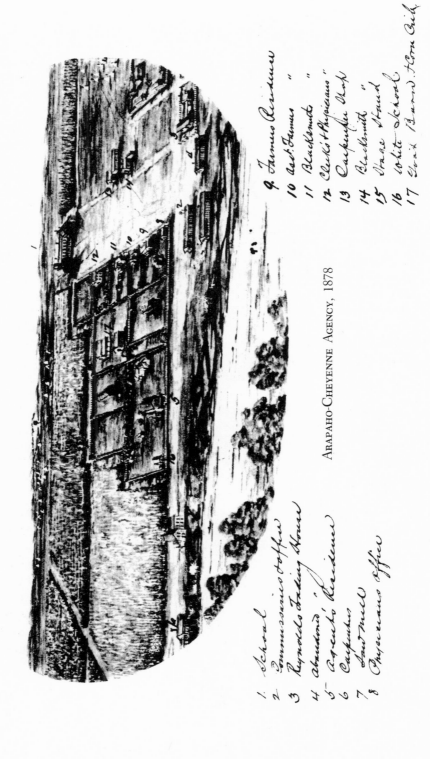

ARAPAHO-CHEYENNE AGENCY, 1878

1. School
2. Commissaries offices
3. Reynolds Fating House
4. Warehouse
5. Agent's Residence
6. Carpenter
7. Surgeon
8. Physicians office

9. Farmers Residence
10. Asst Farmer "
11. Blacksmith "
12. Clerk's Physicians "
13. Carpenters Shop
14. Blacksmith "
15. Horse Stand
16. White School
17. Gout [Gomn] Farm Corral

of white gold-seekers pouring in to found Denver, proved the treaty
false.

Soon after, in the election year of 1864, a rabid ex-elder of the
Methodist Episcopal Church running for election as a delegate to
Congress, gave the *coup de grâce* to the two dispossessed tribes. He
was John M. Chivington, appointed colonel of the 100-day Colorado
Volunteers. Leading his troops to a village of some five hundred
Arapaho and Cheyenne on Sand Creek, comprised mostly of women
and children protected by a handful of men, he attacked without
warning at dawn. The massacre was almost complete. Chivington
rode back to Denver to parade his victorious cavalry through the
streets with their bloody scalps, and to exhibit captured children in
a carnival. This "foul and dastardly crime," as a congressional com-
mittee called it, ended forever the resistance of a broken people.

Three years later, by the terms of a treaty made at Medicine
Lodge, Kansas, the Arapaho and Cheyenne agreed to accept con-
finement on a Reservation between the Canadian and Red rivers in
Oklahoma. Then this treaty too was broken in 1887 by the General
Allotment Act. It provided that each of the few remaining members
of the tribes be assigned a quarter-section of land, the remaining
"surplus" of four and a half million acres being bought by the government for $1.25 an acre and thrown open to white settlers.

This is the unmentioned background for the present memoirs
of Carl Sweezy, as related to Althea Bass. He was born in 1881,
before the Allotment Act was passed; and his is the account of the
Arapaho's detour from the "buffalo road" to the "corn road," their
transition from the Indian to the white way of life.

What gives this small book stature is its complete lack of bitterness and defeatism. It has no trace of the repressed suspicion and
hatred of the white that still characterizes the Hopi, the secrecy of
the Pueblo, the sharp aggressiveness of the Navajo. The Arapaho
emerge from these pages as a people who accepted defeat and change
with courage and proud humility.

Nostalgia is here, for Sweezy was born in a tipi and knew the
old way of life he painted and described so vividly. But he writes
of almost every Army officer, Agent, Mennonite missionary, poli-

tician, visitor, and white neighbor with kindness, tolerance, and a subtle humor. There is no sentimentalizing; there are only facts of life to be faced and accepted. This is the Indian way.

To all of us who now travel together a new and common road, it is beginning to be plain that although the fast-riding, war-bonneted shapes of the past have vanished over the horizon, the spirit that moved them still infuses this land and people with something indestructible, irreplaceable, and uniquely American.

1. AN INDIAN PRIEST.

Courtesy of The Oklahoma Historical Society.

2. PIPE DANCE.

Courtesy of The Oklahoma Historical Society.

3. FIGHTING INDIANS.

4. A Chief.

Courtesy of The Oklahoma Historical Society.

5. THREE CHEYENNE WARRIORS.

Courtesy of Oscar B. Jacobson.

1

These Were
the Arapaho

MY PEOPLE, THE ARAPAHO, are scattered now. There are fewer than one thousand of us who are full-bloods now living in Oklahoma, and many of us who are left do not know our language or our old ways and our old songs and stories. The Cheyenne-Arapaho Agency at Darlington is gone; Fort Reno, across the river from the old Agency, is no longer a fort; our white lodges no longer stand in circles on the prairie with their poles pointed toward the blue sky. Mornings and evenings no smoke from hundreds of campfires rises into the air; no coyotes howl at night and no prairie dogs build their towns on the uplands. No ponies graze in herds on the open ranges. There are fences dividing the farms, and barns for the cows and horses, and roads marking the land in sections, and highways carrying the people in fast cars from one town to another or from town to their farm homes. A pony carrying an Indian woman on its back, with a travois dragging behind to carry the children and the puppies and the household goods to the hunt or to another village, is never seen.

A boy growing up today has no way of knowing how good life was on the Cheyenne-Arapaho Reservation when I was a boy, or what that life was like, unless he reads about it in books. Even if he should read books about our life, he would miss something. Books could not make him see the sun rising over the land that stretched for miles without fences or roads, or the North Canadian River and

the smaller streams winding through that land with trees and brush
along their banks and reeds and grass as high as a man's waist in
the low places, or feel how friendly the life in our villages was, with
children and dogs and ponies outside the tipis, and men and women
busy drying meat or beading moccasins or making arrows or dressing skins. But I am an old man who can remember all this from
my boyhood, before the white man's government and religion and
houses and inventions changed everything. The road of the Arapaho was an old and good one, and we believed it had been traveled
since the beginning of the world. Now, though we can no longer
travel it, it is a good thing to show how that road once ran before
we lost it.

In the beginning, we Arapaho called ourselves by a different
name that meant "Our Own Kind of People." We had our own
kind of lodges and dress, our own societies and beliefs and ways of
worship. The Cheyenne called us "Cloud Men," and the Sioux
called us "Blue Clouds." We believed that we were the first people
created, and that when we were made we were placed in the center
of the earth. That was convenient, because we were traders and
exchanged goods with all the other Indian tribes around us. The
word "Arapaho" means trader. We lived all over the Great Plains,
as far west as the Rocky Mountains and east beyond the Mississippi,
in the beginning. We hunted and traded there, and got along well
with most of the other tribes and held our own against those who
were our enemies. After the white men came to the Plains, some of
us moved farther south and were separated from the rest of our tribe.
Since then we have been called the Southern Arapaho. We never
quarreled with the northern division of our tribe, or had any differ-
ences with them in our beliefs; we are still one people and we like
to visit them in Wyoming and have them visit us in Oklahoma.

My people were always known to be friendly and peace-loving.
But we had our great war chiefs and our weapons and our dances
for war, and when we had to fight we fought hard and well. Long
before my day we had been at war with the Ute and the Shoshoni,
and when I was a boy we still spoke of the Navajo and the Pawnee
as our enemies. But when we made peace, with Indians or with

white men, we mean it and we kept it. When our great chief Little Raven signed the treaty at Medicine Lodge, we agreed not to make war again and to sit down on the Reservation with the Cheyenne in what is now Oklahoma. Little Raven saw that the old days were ended, and that we must live at peace with the white men who were coming to the Great Plains with guns and wagons and cattle and machinery. He gave his promise, and we have kept it. Later, when the white men moved their camps to our Reservation and hunted there, or stole our cattle and horses, or held back the rations they had promised to provide for us until we learned to live as they lived, we did not go to war.

Since long before the white man came, the Cheyenne and the Arapaho had followed much the same road. We had been joined together against our common enemies and so had made war together; our religion, our stories, our way of doing things in camp and on the hunt and the warpath were much alike. But the Cheyenne had outnumbered us for a long time. They had always been more war-like and proud than we were, and perhaps that is why there were more of them. After we sat down on the Reservation, they still out-numbered us something like two to one, and they continued to be prouder and less willing to accept the white man's rule than we were. They insisted on having their own dealings with missionaries and traders and the Agent, and they would never send their chil-dren to the same school with ours. Maybe that was a good thing; maybe that is the reason each tribe has kept some of its own ways and beliefs to this day.

Our languages were different. To us, Cheyenne was full of harsh, sharp sounds, while Arapaho was soft and sounded musical. Hardly anyone in either tribe knew the language of the other. People who studied them said that, while we belonged to what they called the same language group, Arapaho was much harder to learn than Cheyenne, and that Arapaho was one of the most difficult of all the Indian languages. But to us Arapaho, it was not hard; we learned it just as we learned to ride horseback and dance and swim and sing. When we talked with the Cheyenne, we used the sign language. All the Plains Indians knew this language, and talked in it with their hands as fast as they could speak in their own. It was English that was hard for us to learn. Only a few people, like the Cheyenne Paul Boynton, who interpreted at the Agency when I was a boy there, knew both Cheyenne and Arapaho and could interpret them in good English.

President Grant was the Great White Father in Washington when we came to the Reservation. Before that time he had been a great warrior, just as our chiefs Left Hand and Powder Face had been, but he had left the warpath and he wanted us to leave it. So he saw to it that good men were sent to take charge of our Agency, and good officers and soldiers to Fort Reno when it was built across the river from the Agency in 1875. There was more than one white man's road that we might take, and President Grant wanted us to take the right one.

He sent Brinton Darlington to be our first Agent. Mr. Darlington belonged to the Society of Friends, the Quakers, and we could tell that he believed many of the things that we believed. He knew, as we did, that there was a good Man-Above and an evil Man-Below, and he worshipped and prayed to the Man-Above. And although he never spoke to my people about his belief in Mother-Earth, he must have believed in her as we did. He and the men he brought with him had strong power in planting and harvesting, while we depended on what Mother-Earth gave us, growing wild. He never spoke to us about the power of the Four Old Men, that comes from the four quarters of the earth, or of the mysteries of Grandfather Sun that lights the day, or of the Moon the Night-Sun, or of the influences of buffalo and eagle and owl and coyote. He had not been trained in our religious societies and did not know our ceremonies. But he did not try to wipe them all out, as some white people believed in doing.

Brinton Darlington came to the Agency as our friend and helper, and we liked him. At first he was at Camp Supply, an old Army base, but after going over the Reservation with some of our chiefs he built the Agency at a place on the North Canadian River, a few miles from where El Reno now stands. It was a good location, on the old Traders' Trail that was a branch of the Chisholm Trail, where the river bed was wide and sandy and the land level and rich and clear of brush. Later the place was named Darlington, in his honor. He brought assistants there, many of them Quakers like himself, who built good buildings and started schools and opened trading posts and laid out farms. He planted an orchard and a garden, so that our people might learn how fruits and vegetables grew. He was patient and kind; he managed like a chief; he prayed to the Man-Above when he was thankful and when he needed power. So although he was a white man and did not speak our language, we could understand him. He died in 1872, some years before I was born, and when he was buried in the cemetery on the hill near the road that ran between the Agency and Caddo Spring, there were Cheyenne and Arapaho chiefs, as well as white men, who wept over his grave. And when John D. Miles came to be our next Agent, we kept to the new road that we had taken under Brinton Darlington. Even today, when the Arapaho think of Darlington we think of a place where life was once happy and good.

We had everything to learn about the white man's road. We had come to a country that was new to us, where wind and rain and rivers and heat and cold and even some of the plants and animals were different from what we had always known. We had to learn to live by farming instead of by hunting and trading; we had to learn from people who did not speak our language or try to learn it, except for a few words, though they expected us to learn theirs. We had to learn to cut our hair short, and to wear close-fitting clothes made of dull-colored cloth, and to live in houses, though we knew that our long braids of hair and embroidered robes and moccasins and tall, round lodges were more beautiful.

Every white man seemed to have a great concern about time. We had our own names for the seasons and for the months that made up the year, but they were not the same as those the white man used. And we did not know how he counted time, by minutes and hours and days of the week, or why he divided the day into such small parts. And we found that there were two ways of counting it, for the Quakers spoke of First-day, Second-day, and Third-day, and of First-month, Second-month, and Third-month, while others spoke of Sunday and Monday and Tuesday, and of January and February and March.

We had never made brick or sawed lumber or had a wooden door to open and shut. Although some of us had visited the forts and the trading posts before we came to the Reservation, and a few of us had seen the white man's towns and cities, hardly any of us had ever been in houses where families lived. We thought windows were put in the walls so that we might look in to see how white people did their work and ate their meals and visited with each other. We pulled up some of the first little trees that were planted at Darlington, to see why the white people had put sticks in the ground in rows. There is a story that one of our men, given a little pig to raise so that when it grew up he could have pork and bacon, returned it to the Agency to be kept for him until it grew too big to get through the holes in his fence. He did not realize that he could repair the fence to suit the size of his pig.

We knew nothing about how to harness a work horse or turn a furrow in a field or cut and store hay; and today I suppose there are men living in cities who know no more about these things than we did. Our women did not know how to build a fire in a cook-stove or wash clothes in a tub of water. It was a long time before we knew what the figures on the face of a clock meant, or why people looked at them before they ate their meals or started off to church. We had to learn that clocks had something to do with the hours and minutes that the white people mentioned so often. Hours, minutes, and seconds were such small divisions of time that we had never thought of them. When the sun rose, when it was high in the sky, and when it set were all the divisions of the day that we had ever found necessary when we followed the old Arapaho road. When we went on a hunting trip or to a sun dance, we counted time by sleeps.

My people had everything to learn about the white man's road, but they had a good time learning it. How they laughed when a war pony, not understanding what it was supposed to do when it was hitched to a plough or a wagon, lunged and jumped away and threw them flat on the ground, with the plough or the wagon riding high in the air. How puzzled they were when they found that old men and women, among the white people, had teeth they could take out of their mouths and put back in again. They gave Brinton Darlington the name "Tosimeea," "He Who Takes Out His Teeth," when he showed them that he could do this, and they wondered how he had come by that strange power. But when Mr. Miles came, he could do the same thing. It must be, they thought, something all Agents had the power to do; so the movement of taking out and putting back a set of teeth became the word for Agent in our sign language. And stair steps, built to take people up to a house built on top of another house, still amused us. We had never expected to have such things for our own use, on our Reservation.

Slowly, the Cheyenne and the Arapaho began to understand some of these things. But when I was a boy at Darlington they were still only beginning to learn. Most of them kept to the old way, in family and village and tribe, and there are a few of us left who can still remember it. We can remember the stretches of prairie where we rode and hunted, mile after mile with no one to stop us; we can remember our villages of tipis, with a crier calling the day's news from one village to the next in the evening quiet; we can remember annuity and issue days, when we dressed in our best robes and moccasins and gathered on the Agency grounds to visit together and receive the goods and the food we needed until we learned to earn money and raise crops and cattle in the white man's way. We can remember our great summer dances, when our whole tribe gathered and put up the medicine lodge and sang and danced and prayed and visited, and made our vows to the Man-Above and received our blessings. Even today, when we pass some spot that is now Geary or Bridgeport or Greenfield, we stop and say, "This is the place where we built the medicine lodge and held the Sun Dance, that summer when we were boys. Remember?"

2

The Family Tipi

I HAVE NEVER KNOWN the date of my birth, and I never had a birth-day party in my childhood. This was true of all Indian children that I knew when I was growing up, and did not mean that our parents were lacking in love and attention toward us, but only that they knew nothing about dates and had no way of recording them. They usually gave a feast when a new baby was named and one when he first began to walk; and they and our older relatives and friends taught us all we were supposed to know about good manners and the right way to live. We never doubted that they loved us and were concerned for us, even though our birthdays were never celebrated. White people have looked into our school records and tell me I was probably born in 1881, because they find me listed as a child of seven at the Mennonite Mission School in 1888. But I do not know the month or the date of my birth.

The first thing I remember about my childhood is the tipi where my family lived. It was one of many that belonged to our band or village, and was always somewhere not far from the Agency. All of our tipis were a good deal alike, and yet none of us children ever made the mistake of getting into the wrong one when we wanted to go home to our mothers, perhaps for the same reason that prairie dogs never ran into the wrong hole in the ground or cliff swallows never flew into the wrong opening in the river bank. We were within sound of the big bell that hung above the stable at the Agency and was rung at seven in the morning and at noon and at six in the evening, to tell the employees there when to go to work and when to stop. On good days, too, we could hear the bugle calls from Fort Reno, a mile and a half away from the Agency on the high land across the Canadian River. For us in our villages, these bells and bugle calls served as clocks when we needed to take notice of time in the white man's way.

Except in midwinter, most of us were stirring in our village long before we heard the Agency bell ring seven o'clock. Our circle of lodges was open to the east, and each one of the lodges within the circle also opened eastward, to the dawn of light and to the sunrise. That was the way the Arapaho had been taught to build their lodges, at the beginning of time, and that was the way we had always built them. I never saw an Arapaho tipi facing any other way, and if I had seen one, even when I was very small, I would have known that something, or everything, about it was wrong.

When I was born, most of the Cheyenne and the Arapaho still lived in tipis. Brinton Darlington, when he first came to the Agency, had called our chiefs together and told them he wanted them to live as white people lived, in houses with gardens and orchards and fields around them. The Government, he said, would help us build our houses when we were ready to live in them. But this meant a great change, and one we could not make in a hurry. We liked our tipis, with all our things around us in a circle. I have heard white people talk, of late, about the modern circular house, with arrangements for heat and plumbing in the center, new as tomorrow, they say. Well, ours were circular, with a central fire, but I never heard an Arapaho boast that the idea was a new one.

The corn road, we found, was different from the buffalo road in more ways than anyone, white or Indian, had realized, and the old people could not learn it in a hurry. But in 1872 a man named John Seger was hired to come to Darlington, to set up a sawmill and a brick plant, and to help build houses and school buildings and offices and a commissary there. He built good buildings, some of them three stories high, and we liked him. He lived among the Cheyenne and the Arapaho for more than fifty years, building and teaching and farming and running a stage and mail line, and he was our friend until he died at Colony in 1928. His children played with

us and went to our Arapaho school and learned our language and
songs and games and stories. Some people said they even came to
look like us.

Mr. Seger had a fine memory, and he liked to tell stories about
interesting and amusing things that happened on the Reservation.
One of the stories he liked to tell was that of how Little Raven
objected to the house the Agent proposed to build for him on the
Reservation. Little Raven had been taken East, with some other
chiefs of the Cheyenne and the Arapaho, to meet the Great White
Father and to see the wonders of Washington and Philadelphia and
other cities. The house of the Great White Father was big and fine,
he said, and so were the houses of many other people living there.
Since he was one of the principal chiefs of the Arapaho, as the President was the principal chief of the white people, would the Agent
see that his house was built like the White House in Washington?
Such a house, the Agent explained, would cost too much money.
Little Raven, enjoying the argument, answered that money was made
in Washington; he had been taken to the United States Mint and
had seen it made. Would the Agent send word to the Mint to make
enough money to build him a house like that of the President? There
was a good deal of fun over that argument, and Little Raven enjoyed
it as much as the others did. Later, he accepted one of the Government buildings at Cantonment as his house, and he ploughed and
planted some of the land around it. But he kept a tipi in his yard,
and when he longed for the old ways that were passing, he could
stay there.

In the winter, our villages stood on low, sheltered ground near
the river, where the wind and cold could not reach us; in summer
they were moved to higher ground where they could catch the cool
winds. We could not only move our houses but could move entire
villages, and we often did. In this respect we were better off than
the white man is. We moved to suit the seasons, in summer or in
winter; we moved to be near a good supply of wood and water, or
for fresh pasture for our ponies. All the Reservation, nearly four and
a half million acres, was open and free, except for the ground set
aside for the Agency and for Fort Reno. To us who were young, its

streams and thickets and prairies seemed to stretch to the end of the world, but when we listened to the talk of the old men and women we knew they considered the Reservation small and the white settlements too close to us. When I was little, one of the old women who visited with us in our tipi used to tell us how far the Arapaho traveled in her childhood, hundreds of miles in every direction, hunting deer and buffalo and dressing and trading their skins. She remembered the Black Hills in South Dakota and the country around them, and said it all belonged by right to the Arapaho. She had been born there, and had lived there as a little girl.

The buffalo had all gone from our Reservation when I was born, but our band could still go on the hunt for smaller game and stay for weeks, bringing home skins of bear and beaver and wildcat and coon and wolf and deer and badger. These we sold to the traders at the Agency. Fences and farms were only beginning to change the look of the Reservation, in my childhood.

I suppose any family's goods could be packed and the tipi taken down for a move in an hour or two. The mother kept the robes and moccasins in heavy skin holders, called parfleches, that were heavier and stiffer than a bag and made like a little trunk; and she kept her few pots and kettles and cooking supplies in two or three boxes that she had got from one of the traders. These, and some skins and low bed frames and willow-rod mattresses that were thin and light enough to roll up easily, were all we had to move except the tipi itself.

We never had too much around when I was little; we needed less than people have today. I don't think any Arapaho family had a set of dishes, but we didn't need them for our simple meals. Meat cooked in a big iron pot with vegetables, when we had them, and bread and coffee, made a fine meal. For this food there was some kind of plate for every member of the family, made of polished wood or tin or china, a spoon that might be either horn or metal, and some kind of cup. If a family gave a feast, those that came to it brought their own utensils. Even today, at an Indian gathering, the family or the organization giving it usually announces that the food will be served Indian style. That means "bring your own dishes."

The woman of the family had built the lodge, and when we

went to a new location she was the one that moved it. We had no architects and no carpenters; we used no nails and needed no saws or hammers to put up our houses. Raising or striking a tipi was not such heavy work as people who have never seen it done suppose it to be, but it was work that needed training and skill. It needed what white people watching it done called know-how. It was women's work, as it always had been, and they took great pride in it. The important thing, besides the know-how, was the lodge poles. These must be long and straight and slender, and for a good family lodge there must be from sixteen to twenty of them. They must be of some wood like cedar that would not rot when they were exposed to rain and snow. Such poles were not easy to find on the Plains, and the women took great care of them.

An Arapaho woman, in putting up a tipi, started with three poles that she bound together about three feet from the small end. These she set up on the ground like a big tripod. Then she propped more poles on the ground and rested them above in the fork of the first three. These were spaced evenly in a circle and formed the framework of the tipi. Many buffalo skins sewed together had once made the cover for this frame, but the old lodge skins soon wore out after the buffalo were gone, and then a heavy cloth called lodge cloth or strouding was used. This cloth was cut and sewed in such a way that it formed a kind of cone stretched over the poles. Yet it was not exactly a cone, for two flaps, or ears, were left open at the top, with two more poles thrust through them in such a way that they made the smoke hole above the center of the lodge large or small, depending on how they were braced on the ground. These could be adjusted according to how much wind blew and in what direction.

Above the entrance, the cone-shaped canvas was fastened together with wooden pegs about the way an overcoat is fastened with big buttons. The opening that made the entrance was covered with a skin or a length of canvas held down by a strip of wood that weighted the bottom. This was the only kind of door we knew, long ago. In fine weather it was raised on poles to make a kind of awning over the opening. This door could not be locked, of course, like a wooden door on hinges; but the Cheyenne and the Arapaho, like

most other Indians, had always respected other people's houses and
never molested them. When they were away from the tipi for any
length of time, they placed a stick across the entrance to say that
they were not at home. It was not so tight as the locks people have
on their doors today, but it made things safer. Our sense of honor
protected our property.

Our tipis did not need paint as houses made of lumber did.
They were white, except for a brown stain at the top made by the
smoke from our fires. The tipis of the Cheyenne and the Arapaho
were taller than those of other Indians. Anyone traveling the prairies
long ago knew one of our villages as soon as he saw it, even before
he was near enough to recognize the people or the designs on the
chief's tent or the shields and trophies hanging outside. The low,
round lodges of other tribes were never so beautiful as ours; they
never stood so white and tall, with the poles crossed so high against
the sky, as ours.

In a family tipi, everything was neat and orderly. Right by the
entrance, as one came in from the east, were the boxes from the
trader's store, where sugar and salt and flour and coffee were kept.
These things by the door were white man's goods. Beyond that, the
furnishings and their arrangement were just as the Arapaho had
always had them, made in the old way and placed in the lodge as
they had been from the beginning. Our styles in furnishing never
changed in the old days. The beds were always around the edge of
the circle, and a well-furnished lodge usually had three, one on the
south, one on the west, and one on the north. The bed was made
of a low wooden frame, with a kind of mattress made of willow twigs
laid over it. These twigs were straightened and peeled and polished,
and held together by leather thongs run through holes bored near
the end of each twig. The mattress was longer than the bed, and
narrowed at one or both ends, where it was held up by a kind of
tripod to make a back-rest. Painted or rubbed to a high polish, these
back-rests looked very fine. Over them, and over the bed itself, robes
and skins were laid, and in later years woven blankets, to make a
comfortable place to sit during the day and for a covering at night.

As you entered the tipi and turned to the left, the first bed belonged to the women of the family. Then the western part of the lodge, opposite the entrance, belonged especially to the father. Here, on a pole or a tripod, were hung his painted shield and his quiver of arrows; here he kept the bundle, wrapped in skin, containing the things that were his particular protection and power, things that the rest of the family never used or handled; and here he kept his saddle. Here was his bed, with its back-rests and robes, where he sat when he worked or entertained his friends; and behind the bed on the wall of the tipi he might have a finely dressed skin painted with designs and figures that represented important happenings and influences in his life. Beyond this, on the north side of the tipi, was the third bed, where the boys in the family slept and where visitors usually sat. A specially honored visitor, or one whose friendship with the father was close, might sit with him on his bed, at his left. When the family entered the tipi, they turned to the left, while a visitor went to the right.

The floor in the center of the lodge was bare earth, scraped smooth and clean; but around the outside of the circle, where the beds were and where the wall of the tipi slanted against them, the grass might be left to cover the ground. Below the smoke hole, a small place was dug out of the ground and lined with stones. Here our fire burned, for heat and for cooking, with the sticks of wood all laid flat and pointing in toward the center, to be pushed farther in as they burned. It is surprising how small a fire was needed even when there was snow on the ground outside. The mother in the family set her cooking pot on the stones or hung it from a stout forked stick above the fire, and some food was always simmering there. Behind this central fire, some stones were laid for a smaller one, which was sacred. Here our offerings to the Man-Above were placed; here, when cedar or sage was burned, such objects as my father's shield or my mother's ceremonial robe or a bundle of arrows were purified and blessed. When we smelled the clean odor burning there, we felt that our home and everything in it had been blessed.

There was room for everything in our lodge, and to us it never seemed crowded. Bags of meat and fruit that my mother had dried hung from the lodge poles, out of our way; and around the outer circle of the room, in the space where the beds were and underneath them, folded robes and clothing, our toys, and our mother's tools and materials for handwork were kept. Some of these were laid in parfleches, so that they could be kept clean and handled easily. Except in bad weather, most of our work and play went on outside our tipi. When we came inside, it seemed dim and cool in summer, and rosy and warm in winter. A kettle of food was usually on the fire, ready for us and for any visitors who might come in. It was unheard of among us for visitors to come and leave unfed, as long as there was anything to be had to eat. Sometimes we children brought white playmates, children of Agency employees, to our tipis, knowing our parents would welcome them and make them feel at home, even though the visitors could not speak Arapaho and our parents could speak little or no English. When there is true hospitality, not very many words are needed. Every Arapaho child learned this.

The women in our tribe were naturally good housewives. People who laugh at them and say they were dirty and untidy forget how little they had to work with and how much they had to learn when they changed from the buffalo road to the corn road. When I was little, we took for granted our orderly tipis, the kettle of food always ready to eat, and the extra moccasins stored away to replace the ones we wore out. Later I learned, when I went into the world to school and to work, that there are many kinds of housewives, some good and some bad. But the Arapaho women had a gift for making their lodges homelike and caring for their families and showing hospitality. That was why, when schools and teachers came to our Agency, our girls and women took up the white women's way of doing things and did them well. They had always made beautiful moccasins and belts and robes and leggings, decorated with fine quillwork or with beads. For this work they had used awls made of bone or horn or thorn, and stout string made of deerskin or sinew. Sewing on cloth, with needles and thread and sometimes with a sewing machine to do the stitching, came easy after this. And so did laundering and baking and cleaning, when there were soap and milled flour and iron stoves and straw brooms to make use of.

In winter, there were windbreaks to shelter our lodges. The women went to the river in the fall and cut a kind of tall grass that grew in low, wet places along the edge of the water. It grew like reeds or cattails, and we called it otter grass because otters lived among the roots and made their nests there. The women bound this grass into panels and set them up like a stockade fence outside our tipis, to shut out the wind and the snow. Then they pegged down the lodge cloth and laid sod or earth over it to seal it. When that was done, we were snug for the winter, however stormy it might be outside.

Winter or summer, our village made a beautiful sight when the sun went down, with the crossed poles pointing up into the dark sky and the fire in the center of each lodge turning it into a big cone of light, with shadows from the furnishings and the people moving about. Sometimes a bell tinkled, where a herd of ponies grazed; sometimes dogs barked, before they settled down for the night; often there was a drum beating, deep and slow or fast and sharp. Sometimes there was the sound of a flute, playing two or three notes over and over, or of men and women singing around a campfire. In the distance there were lights at the Agency and at the Fort, and beyond them the prairie stretched away in the darkness, mile after mile.

6. INSIDE A FAMILY TIPI.

7. An Indian Warrior.

8. OKLAHOMA DANCERS.

Courtesy of Oscar B. Jacobson.

9. A War Dan

3

Chiefs
and Headmen

WHITE PEOPLE who did not try so hard to understand the ways of
the Cheyenne and the Arapaho as we did to understand their ways,
thought we were all lazy. That was because we took a different atti-
tude toward time from theirs. We enjoyed time; they measured it.
Our women did not say, on Monday (or on Second-day, as the
Quakers put it) we wash our clothes; on Tuesday we iron them;
on Saturday we bake and clean; on Sunday we do no work and we
go to church. Our men did not say, after breakfast, at eight o'clock
I go to my schoolroom, or to my office, or to the commissary; at twelve
I go home to my dinner; at one I go back to work all afternoon. They
did not say, this week we break sod and plough; next week we plant
our corn or our potatoes and melons and cabbage.

For hundreds of years we had gone on a long hunt twice a
year, whenever our scouts had come in to report that buffalo were
plenty out on the Plains; we had held our buffalo dance before we
left, and had set out with our best bows and arrows, our shields and
lances for protection from our enemies if we should meet with any
of them, and pemmican for food to eat until we killed meat. We had
taken our women and children along because they too loved to move
over the prairies, making camp where grass was green and water
fresh, and because our women must skin the animals and dress the
hides and dry the meat where we killed it. No Sundays could be

set aside for church or rest, or Mondays for washing, when we followed the buffalo road. And we had no set date for coming back,
for that depended on the buffalo and on the weather. When we had
meat enough and the skins were dry enough to pack, we started back
to the home camp.

But we were not an idle nation of people. If we had been idlers,
we would have been wiped out by our enemies, or by bad weather
and starvation long ago. Before our Reservation days, we had hunted
and traded over the land that makes up many states now—the Da-
kotas and Utah and Wyoming and Nebraska and Kansas and Colorado—and there are stories of raids that we made with other tribes of
the Plains as far south as Mexico. Those were brave, free days. We
had no time, and no need, to plant crops or raise corn and hogs and
chickens, or build houses and barns like the white man's then. But
when we followed the buffalo road we worked hard, just as white
people who followed the corn road worked hard. No people who get
their living from Mother-Earth as she provides it for them, and who
fight off other tribes wanting to hunt and graze their horses over the
same land, can be lazy.

Foremost among us were our chiefs. Four of these were principal chiefs, heading the four divisions of the Southern Arapaho;
under these were sub-chiefs, one for each of our bands or villages.
Our chiefs were chosen by the people, not born to hold their office
as kings are born. They served for life, unless they failed to perform
their duties in a way that satisfied the people. If they did wrong or
lost the confidence of the people, they could resign or be deposed
to make way for someone else. They had to be men who could lead
their village or the whole tribe, and make decisions for them. They
had to do something more than wear a fine shirt and leggings and
moccasins while they rode a fiery war horse and carried a decorated
lance and shield. If the tribe must move, because white people were
too near or Indian enemies were taking too big a share of the game
and the grazing, they must decide where we were to go and conduct
us there safely. They must decide when war must be made; and
when it had been decided on, they saw that all the people were

notified and the ceremonies for going to war carried out and the safety of the women and children planned for.

When peace was made, they sat in council and made the terms of settlement with the enemy; they saw to it that the proper prayers and ceremonies for peace were offered, and that all the tribe were of one mind to keep it. When we made a peace agreement, we meant it; our chiefs and priests, as well as our warriors, studied and prayed and talked over the terms of peace and held religious ceremonies to make these terms solemn and binding. If some of our leaders were hot-headed when a peace conference began, they were cool and in a religious frame of mind by the time an agreement had been reached. Our peace treaties lasted.

All four of our principal chiefs were present at the treaty of Medicine Lodge in 1867: Little Raven, Spotted Wolf, Yellow Bear, and Powder Face. They had spoken well there; they had made the white man understand that we wanted peace and meant to keep it, and that to keep peace our people must have a reservation of their own, where white people and other Indian tribes would not interfere with us. Little Raven's speeches at the Council of Medicine Lodge are remembered, even today, by Indians and white men alike. He was an old man still living on the Reservation when I was born, but I was too young to know him except as a little boy admiring a great man. He died at Cantonment in 1889. What I remember best about him is the stories our elders told of the power of his oratory and the wise, sharp way he had of thinking. It was not his work to plough and plant and hoe, or to raise cattle and hogs, as most of the rest of us were learning to do. Those were not things that a leader of the people, in war and in councils, had ever done among the Arapaho. To be our kind of leader, he had to spend much time talking and listening, and thinking and contemplating. By these means he could look at things clearly and fairly. He was what white people would call a statesman and a philosopher.

At Medicine Lodge, it is said, the Indian Commissioner, N. G. Taylor, talked to Little Raven about the white man's religion. There is a heaven above, he said, where all good men go, white people and Indians alike, after they die, and a hell where all evil men go.

Those who lie and cheat and break their promises may not go to
this heaven above, Mr. Taylor said. At this Little Raven laughed
until he was out of breath. That is a good thing to know, he told
Mr. Taylor when he had finished laughing. Remembering all the
broken promises and greed and cruelty of the white man in his dealings with the Indians, he said that he supposed heaven must be a
place where Indians would not be much troubled by white people.
There would be few of them that Little Raven would expect to
see there.

Little Raven went about among the people on the Reservation,
advising and encouraging them. He told them he was too old to
learn to set figures· down in a book or to read and write English
words, but he knew that all who were young enough must go to
school and learn to do those things. He opposed gambling and drinking because he saw that they made trouble. Once he came upon
some of our village chiefs gambling with the Cheyenne. He broke
up the game, and took the Arapaho men to one side to tell them
why he had interfered. Gambling, he said, led to quarreling, and
if the Arapaho quarreled with the proud, unsociable Cheyenne they
would soon reach the stage of war between the two tribes, on their
own Reservation. The Arapaho never forgot that speech, and there
was never much gambling among them, even by the younger men.
When Little Raven walked through a camp, wearing his fine robes,
with his long hair bound with otter skins, moving slowly and proudly
as an old man of importance has a right to do, they could see that he
was a leader. At his home they knew he had, ready to wear for any
ceremony, his panther-skin quiver dressed with the claws on and
filled with arrows, some of which he had taken from enemies he had
killed long ago when he was a warrior.

Powder Face was one of the great old-time chiefs that I can
remember at Darlington. He was a real leader in taking up the new
road laid out for us by the white man. He set the example by raising
corn and planting a garden and setting out fruit trees. But he often
had bad luck with his corn because of floods or dry weather, or by
having fences around his fields burned in a prairie fire and his crops
destroyed by livestock that got in to them. Because of this bad luck

in the early years, he came to believe that, on much of our Reservation, the cattle road would be a better one to follow than the corn road. He soon built up a fine herd of cattle, and put his own brand on them just as the white man did. His brand was the circle-bar-circle. He published this brand in the *Cheyenne Transporter,* the newspaper published for several years at Darlington, paying to have it published and to have the newspaper sent to him, just as white cattlemen who leased pastures from us on our Reservation did.

Powder Face not only set the example himself but encouraged the rest of us to raise livestock and care for them and sell them, never neglecting them when we wanted to go on a hunt or to hold a medicine dance. For an old warrior who had made a name for himself, even among white soldiers, that was a long road to travel. His father, old Powder Face, had given him his shield years before, when he was about seventeen, and had told him to carry it in battle against the Pawnees. Powder Face had returned from that battle with six Pawnee scalps, and then had been given thirty young warriors over whom he was to be chief. Before he had taken up the white man's road, he had scalped white men as well as Indians. When he related his war story, he told how he had had fifty-five horses shot out from under him by white soldiers, and had been wounded four times. After the treaty of Medicine Lodge, when he left the warpath, he went with white officers to Lawrence, Kansas, where he saw more white men and women and children than he had realized there were in all the world. He knew then that he had been wise to sign the treaty because his people must live in the white man's way or perish. After that, he helped gather the Arapaho villages together, out on the western Plains, and bring them in to sit down on the Reservation. There he encouraged parents to send their children to school and to learn about the white man's religion. He often came to the Sunday school at Darlington to talk to the children there.

It was a fine thing to see Powder Face moving through our camp or along the street at the Agency, a powerful-looking man who knew how to be both firm and friendly. Usually his wife was with him. She was a slender, pretty woman, and she walked by his side instead of behind him in Indian fashion. Some of the Arapaho men, especially the chiefs, had more than one wife, but Powder Face had only one and he treated her with the same kind of courtesy that the best of white men show their wives. When he traveled, she went with him, and they had more than one merry trip together, even going as far as the eastern coast, riding the white man's trains and steamboats. Whenever he dressed for a ceremony, he wore a fine buffalo robe that she had embroidered in beads for him, and a buckskin shirt that had been handed down to him and was ornamented, people said, with hundreds of scalps fastened to the fringe. I never saw the shirt, but I think the people that told about it multiplied the number of scalps. But to Powder Face they were a symbol of bravery, not of cruelty. In the white man's Bible, which he learned about when he went to Sunday school and church at the Mennonite Mission at the Agency, he said there were stories of brave warriors such as he had tried to be.

The principal chief that I remember best from my boyhood was Left Hand. He, too, had been a great war chief. Long before the day of the Medicine Lodge treaty, he had been fired on at Fort Larned when he was trying to make a peace treaty between some of the Plains Indians and the soldiers at the Fort, and he had led the Arapaho in the war that followed. But his heart was good, as well as brave, and he led us in peace on the Reservation just as he had led us in war before. When the Agents at Darlington were Army officers, as they were for some time after the first few years, they recognized him as a military man and a leader. He had a record as a warrior that they could respect, just as Powder Face had. Now it was his duty to leave the warpath behind and make a new road for his people.

Even the way of getting married was different, when we left the buffalo road. Left Hand understood that the old customs of marriage, by which the young man left ponies and other gifts outside his sweetheart's tipi, and her parents, if she chose him, accepted these, did not make a marriage legal according to the white man's law. When his daughter wished to marry, he set the example by having the ceremony performed at the Agency, with a license from the probate judge and a minister to perform the rites. But he kept some of the old Arapaho way, too, in that ceremony. After the minister's prayer, Left Hand also made a prayer. Then he took the hands of his son-in-law and his daughter, touched his heart and his forehead, and blessed them. Each of the Indian guests then took the hands of the couple in theirs while they said a prayer. So the marriage was legal and Christian, and Arapaho as well. The Agent thought this ceremony so impressive that he wrote about it in his report to Washington. Soon many other marriages were performed in this same way. The young man did not have to give up his best ponies; he had only to pay for the marriage license, and the white man's prayers and those of the Indian went up together to the Man-Above. It was a good ceremony.

To Left Hand, and to all the Arapaho, these things were important. We had always been devoted to our women and children, even though our family life and our manners toward them were different from those of the white man. It is true that some of our leading men brought more than one wife to the Reservation. Big Mouth is said to have had seven wives. Yet for his kindness and patience in leading his people along the new road, no man earned more praise from the white Agents and preachers and teachers than Big Mouth. I have been told that in many countries, long ago, men had several wives, and some of the men that we read about in the Bible did. In those times, and in the day when we followed the buffalo road, there was often more work in a home than one woman could do. We never had slaves or servants, and a fighter with much war gear or a chief who had many visitors needed more woman-help in his home than his wife could give him. Men with several wives usually had separate tipis for them, unless they were sisters, and tried to keep them friendly with each other. After we moved to the Reservation and our women had less hard work for their families, and after the white people kept insisting that our marriage customs were bad and illegal, few of our men married more than one wife; but they saw no reason to give up the extra ones they already had.

Besides our principal chiefs, we had our village chiefs or headmen. Each chief knew all the families in his village so well that he could advise them and look after them. When someone was sick, he made sure that the medicine man was called; when some family met with misfortune, he saw that they had food and shelter and clothing. He led his band on the long hunt and on the move. He sent criers through the village, to give out news and to issue orders. He was busier, and gave better service, than any mayor that I know of today.

Yellow Horse was one of the village chiefs that I remember. He was friendly and sociable; he liked to visit at the Agency and the schools, and was interested in everything he saw there. The people of his band liked him, but Mr. Seger thought he was lazy. Mr. Seger used to tell about what he called Yellow Horse's poultry-raising project. Yellow Horse liked the fried eggs that he had eaten in some of the Agency homes, and was told that, if he would raise chickens, he would be able to have fried eggs at home whenever he wanted them. So he was given a setting hen. He promised that he would not neglect her, even though her chickens would not hatch for many days, and he took her home in a box that he set up at the foot of his bed. The way she kept her eggs warm and turned them in the nest was new and interesting to him, and he spent much of his time watching her. Sometimes, about noon, he went to the Agency to report on his hen and to ask how many more days he must wait until the eggs hatched. If he was lucky, some Agency employee wanting to encourage him to hold out to the end took him to his home and had fried eggs served to him before he went back to his tipi.

Shortly before the eggs were to hatch, Yellow Horse had word that buffalo were plentiful not far away and that he must lead his village on the hunt. But he had given his word that he would not leave his hen. So his people agreed that, if he would provide a feast before they set out, they would go on the hunt without him. Yellow Horse sold his best pony for thirty dollars to spend on the feast, and so fulfilled his promise not to neglect his hen and carried out his duty toward his village. Everyone was satisfied with the arrangement except the people at the Agency, who considered it strange that an Indian important enough to be a village chief could not understand the difference between the value of a horse and the value of a hen.

They forgot to count in the good time that everyone had at the feast and the fun that Yellow Horse had in finding a way to keep his word at the Agency and his standing in his village.

New chiefs were chosen, if there was a vacancy, when the whole tribe gathered together in the summer to build the medicine lodge and hold the Sun Dance. The man who was giving up his office, or some other chief of equal importance if the one whose place was to be filled had died or could not be present, stood up before all the people, facing the new chief, and made a speech. This was to tell the new chief about his responsibilities and to encourage him. The speaker would say something like this: "My friend, you are about to be made a chief. After this you will no longer be a common man. You will stand in a high place, where everyone can see you. Sometimes your people will praise you, and sometimes they will find fault with what you do. Do not be discouraged when they blame you, or ashamed when they laugh at you. Walk straight ahead, and do your best for your people."

Sometimes, during this ceremony, the new chief was given a new name, in memory of some former chief or because of something important or good that he had done. Sometimes he kept the name that he had had before. In any case, he kept in mind the new responsibilities that he had taken on himself, and walked straight ahead.

4

Work in the
Camps

AN ARAPAHO CAMP was always a lively, busy place. That had been
true in the old days when we lived wherever we pleased and had no
white people around us; it was just as true after we sat down at
Darlington to exchange the buffalo road for the corn road. Even
though our women did not have many dishes to wash or much baking and laundry to do, as the white women did, they were busy with
their own kind of housekeeping; and even though the men, for the
most part, farmed only a few acres and raised few cattle and hogs
and chickens, they had work to do for themselves and their families
and their villages, just as they had always had. It seems to me that
they enjoyed their work, while they were doing it, more than men
and women do now. It was all done by hand, with few tools and no
machinery, and they gathered their own materials for whatever they
made or used and for much of what they ate. When they finished a
piece of work, it was all their own doing and something to be proud
of. And everything was sociable and friendly while they worked.
Dogs played around doorways; ponies grazed in the open spaces;
children romped with the dogs and climbed on the ponies; women
sat on the ground sewing moccasins or beading pouches; men straightened arrow wood or strung bows or combed and dressed their long
hair.

Our women were strong and, as the wife of one of the Agents

said, did not know they had backs. Wherever we camped, they carried water from the nearest stream or spring, and wood for our fires. Mornings and evenings, it was a pleasant sight to see them going in groups for water, singing and laughing and talking in our soft, sweet-sounding language. Often they stopped to bathe in the stream before they came back, for they were not hurried and had no set time to finish a task as white women had. Long ago they made buckets of buffalo paunches, dried and hardened, or of skin, and some of these were still in use in my childhood, but tin buckets from the traders were replacing these. They wore knives at their belts, handy for all kinds of work, and carried hatchets, sometimes old stone ones, to chop the wood they gathered, and bound with a leather strap so they could swing it up on their backs. I have been told they could carry as much as three hundred pounds in these bundles, but usually the loads were lighter because our fires were small and they never tried to keep a big supply of wood. The white man, our people used to say, builds a big fire and sits far away from it; the Indian builds a little fire and sits close. Our fires took less wood and made less smoke.

At first, our fathers and mothers made everything we had in our camps. Even after good, honest traders came to the Agency, we were slow to make use of the goods they had to sell. We had very little money to buy with, and little need for most of the things the white people at the Agency and at the Fort bought. As long as we lived in tipis we had no need and no place for stoves and tables and chairs, or for the tools used to build and repair houses and furniture. The little we had, as compared with white people, was necessary and useful, either for our daily living or for our ceremonies. That is why our tipis looked simple and orderly and homelike. The things we made by hand were made to last a long time and were decorated so that we could enjoy using them.

The women were responsible for most of the things in and around our tipis. They were the ones who found and cut and seasoned the lodge poles, and replaced them if they were broken or destroyed. They cut and peeled and put together with sinews the willow rods that made our back-rests, painting them or polishing them until they made the lodge look rich. They hunted up smooth, flat stones for the center fire; they kept bundles of cedar and sage on hand, to sweeten and purify whatever might require it; they went to the woods and over the prairies, gathering the roots and the minerals used in painting and dyeing. Old women had handed on to younger ones, since the beginning, the knowledge of how to find and use what was needed to make our tipis comfortable and beautiful.

As long as the buffalo roamed the plains, it supplied us with nearly everything we needed. That animal had been given to us in the beginning of things, and we had learned then how many uses it had for us. Even though the buffalo herds were gone before I was born, and our meat was smaller game and beef, we still used many things we had kept from the days when we followed the buffalo road. We had never wasted any part of the animal when we killed it: its hide made our lodge coverings, robes for our beds and for clothing, and shields and parfleches; its paunch made pails and bowls; its tail and hooves made ornaments; its horns made spoons and tools; its sinews made stout cords; its flesh and fat and organs, its blood and even the marrow of its bones made our food. We used buffalo chips for our campfires, and the women made a powder from them to use in cleaning and dressing their babies' skin. The cattle that were issued to us on the Reservation and that later we learned to raise for ourselves could never fill all the needs the buffalo had filled.

The women had had a great deal to do when buffalo were killed. As soon as they had skinned the animal, they spread the skin on the ground and pegged it down to stretch and dry. They dressed it with bone and horn tools, to take off all the flesh and to soften it. In summer, when the hair was light, they dressed it off to make soft, fine robes; in winter, when the hair was heavy, they left it on. Even today there are women who have the tools and know-how to dress hides in the old way, but now they have only cowhides and once in a while a deer's hide to dress. The women spent many hours down on their hands and knees working on a hide, but when at last it was fleshed and softened and dried it made the finest and warmest kind of robe. They dressed elk and deer skins, as well as buffalo, to make into shirts and leggings and moccasins. We liked the deep yellow color of smoked elkskin; when it was decorated with designs in dyed quills or beads, it made the most beautiful clothing in the world.

It took our women only a short time to cut up a buffalo or a beef, using the wide knives they carried hung from their belts. The brains and the liver we ate raw, sometimes as soon as the kill was made; then the women put meat and bones into their cooking pots, sometimes with cattail roots and later with vegetables from the garden, and boiled them. The rest of the meat they cut into strips and hung from a pole set up between two forked sticks to dry. Some of this they pounded and mixed with dried fruits and covered with melted tallow. This we called pemmican. It made a fine food, and we never went hungry when we had it.

When the women were not busy with other things, they had handwork to do. The Cheyenne and the Arapaho women made the finest of moccasins. Whether they were made of strong, smoked elkskin or of soft, dressed buckskin, they always fitted the feet they were made for, and were decorated in designs that suited the line of the foot. Green was the favorite color for beadwork among the Cheyenne, while the Arapaho used softer and more varied colors. Without measuring tools or patterns, the women made these same designs in the right proportions for children or grown people, generation after generation. White visitors at Darlington used to ask them where they got their patterns for the designs they used on leggings or armbands or moccasins or garters, and how they transferred the patterns to the skins they worked them on. It was a question that always puzzled the Indian women, for the designs were in their own minds; they had never had patterns like those women now use for embroidery. "It is given to me," was about the only answer an Indian woman could make when she was asked this question, and sometimes she pointed to her forehead and smiled. It was like asking a bird how it flew.

I never wondered that the Indian hated to wear the white man's shoes. Our feet, in moccasins, moved as softly and freely as if they were bare, and were beautiful in motion; in shoes with leather soles, they were stiff and awkward. Even today, a young man coming home from the University to spend Saturday and Sunday with his family puts on his moccasins—most likely a pair his mother made and decorated for him—as soon as he enters the house. Then he is at home again.

There were many other things the Arapaho women made from the skins they dressed. Nearly every man had a fancy leather pouch that his wife had made for him, to hold his pipe and tobacco. This was a long, narrow bag, with a drawstring, and with one side decorated in a fine design of beads or quillwork. For children, there were beautiful little beaded cases for the navel cord and for charms, hung from the hood of the cradle board or fastened in the hair. And for almost everyone there were fans. These were made of feathers, but usually the quills of the feathers were mounted with leather and bound into a round handle that was covered with skin and beaded solidly. Some of these fans, for special ceremonies, must be made of the required kind of feathers—eagle or wild turkey or magpie or crow—shaped and put together in the proper way that had been handed down; others, made only for decoration, could be large or small and with the feathers trimmed and dyed in whatever way the one who made them chose.

Nearly every Arapaho mother had a carrier, or what white people call a cradle board, for her baby. The frame of this carrier was made of wood or stiff hide, wider at the top than at the bottom, and long enough to hold the baby till he was ready to walk. Over this frame was fastened a kind of pouch of dressed skin, a little like a cocoon laced together down the front and open at the top, into which the baby, wrapped in the softest skin from the buffalo calf, or in later years in soft cloth, was put. Usually the skin that covered the carrier was decorated with quill or bead designs. Sometimes a kind of veil was fastened over the top, to let down as a cover for the baby's face when he needed protection from wind or sun. The carrier could be propped against the side of the tipi, indoors or out, while the mother worked, or fastened to her back or to her saddle when she went on a journey. It kept the baby safe from falls or accidents, and comfortable when he traveled. Strapped in his cradle, he learned to look at and listen to everything that went on around him, and he grew straight and strong. Usually older relatives made the cradle board and brought it as a gift to the new baby.

The men, like the woman, made many things by hand. Some men made nothing but arrows, and that was a kind of work that took more skill than most men have today. Once, all our living depended on the skill of our arrow-makers, for without arrows we could not defend ourselves from our enemies or shoot the buffalo and other game that we lived on. Bows could be made of several kinds of wood, depending on how big they were to be and the kind of arrow they were to shoot, but the Osage orangewood was the kind most commonly used because it was tough and would bend without breaking. That is why it is called bow-wood. But for arrows we preferred only one kind of wood. This was a dogwood that is not the same as the variety that bears big, four-petaled flowers in spring, and for some reason that I never knew the Arapaho called it Pawnee wood. The grain is so fine and the wood so hard that it will not split or break off in shooting, as lighter and coarser woods do. Even a crooked piece of Pawnee wood could be made straight when it was peeled and worked and dried.

Sometimes we chewed the wood, where it was knotty or bent, and worked it straight as it dried. Our teeth were the best tools for that work. An arrow-maker, too, often kept deer sinews in his mouth, to soften them. These he used to bind the feathers that he fastened to the arrow near the nock to give it speed and direction, and also to join the arrowhead to the base of the shaft. The sinews hardened and shrank as they dried, and looked like heavy glue.

Sometimes a man painted his arrows with lines of color that were his particular protection, or used wild turkey feathers near the end of the shaft because they always gave power. Small arrows, for children to use to shoot birds and squirrels, were made of one piece of wood, cut down above the arrowhead from the original size for the shaft, and polished and made smooth. A very small fault in an arrow made a big difference in the way it carried. So a man who made arrows had plenty to do, to find and keep on hand a good supply of

Pawnee wood, along with deer sinews and gut and feathers and paint and arrowheads. While I was growing up, bows and arrows were still more in use than guns. It took money to buy a good gun, and then there was sometimes no ammunition to be had for it. But the bow and arrow was a weapon we always had, before the time of guns; we could make it ourselves and we could trust it. Some bows were so big and powerful they could carry an arrow half a mile; others were so light and accurate they could bring down a small bird in flight.

The Cheyenne and the Arapaho never needed saddles for their horses. When they rode for business, they rode bareback, lickety-split, controlling their horses with a rope in the mouth and guiding them with knee pressure. When they used saddles in the old days, it was for show, to dress up the horse so that it looked as fine as the rider. At first, the men made their own saddles. These were of wood, and were high and straight at both the front and the back. The framework looked like a small carpenter's horse turned upside down. Painted with bright colors and designs, with colored streamers of cloth or ornamented buckskin hanging from the front and with wooden stirrups, they looked fine. The earliest saddle blankets that we used were made of skins, but when cloth came into general use we made them of heavy woolen material, sometimes dyed a bright color and decorated with streamers and jingles. A man and his horse, tearing across the prairie or down the main street at Darlington, with hair, mane and tail, and ornaments all streaming on the wind, looked like one animal in motion, made for nothing but beauty and speed.

Every man had to spend a good deal of time making and keeping in good shape the gear he needed for war and for ceremonies. Even though we no longer went to war, we still held our war dances, and all of our men still told their war stories at gatherings where they were expected to tell them. Only a few of our great warriors were entitled to wear the long feather war bonnets that everybody now expects any Indian to wear, whatever his tribe may be or his place in it. Little boys buy cheap imitations of these in the dime stores today. But the old war bonnet was a splendid headdress, which

10. THE MEDICINE LODGE OF THE SUN DANCE.

11. A VILLAGE CHIEF WITH HIS DANCERS.

12. INDIANS ATTACKING BUFFALO HUNTER

13. INDIANS FIGHTING WHITE

Courtesy of The Oklahoma Historical So

14. Scraping a Hide Outside a Family Tipi.

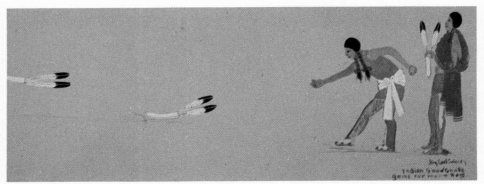

15. INDIAN GAME FOR MEN AND BOYS—SNOW SNAKES.

16. INDIAN GAME FOR BOYS—WHIPPING TOPS.

only Indians of the Plains wore, and then only Indians who had earned the right to wear it. With its rows of eagle feathers fastened in a broad band of decorated buckskin, each feather tipped at the end with a little tassel of dyed horsehair, it was a fine piece of handwork. Another kind of gear that the Arapaho wore was the roach, made of a tail such as that of the beaver or muskrat dyed to a rich color and with a line of wild turkey beards making a kind of crest along the top. These beards glistened and bobbed as the man who wore them moved, and we believed they gave him great power. Once we had all we needed of these beards and prized them highly; now a man is fortunate if he can go hunting and bring back even one.

Lances, too, were bright with decorations. Made of highly polished wood, they were sometimes ornamented with a bunch of eagle feathers mounted on a strip of deerskin in such a way that they streamed on the wind as the warrior carried the lance, and yet were not easily bent or broken. Other lances had a kind of narrow banner of buckskin ornamented with quillwork and feathers and with tassels of dyed horsehair hanging from their whole length. These gave the rider a grand look when his horse was running.

Every warrior had his own specially decorated shield. The toughest part of the buffalo hide was used to make a shield; this, when soaked in water and dried slowly, became so thick and hard that few arrows could go through it. In nearly every village, there was a painter who decorated the shields of the men in his village with the design and in the colors that were each man's special protection and power. All the old shields were marked with black at the rim in four places, to represent the four directions, the Four Old Men. Besides these painted designs, a man's shield could be draped with buckskin and hung with fringes of beads and jingles in any way he wished. At war dances, all these pieces of war gear were brought out and worn or carried. Some of them were very old and had been handed from one man to another for a long time. With war horses running, feathers and banners flying on the wind from spears and lances, shields and quivers shining at men's sides and shoulders, and women singing war songs for their men, I think a war party setting out, or coming in victorious, must have been one of the splendid things in life to see. If I had to miss that, I have had the next best thing: I have seen old warriors wearing their fine trappings, and I have heard them tell their stories.

Priests and medicine men had their work, too. They must gather the roots and herbs that only they knew how to find and use, and prepare the paints they needed for their ceremonies. They must learn the songs and the rites used in healing and in medicine dances, and must teach these things to those who assisted them so that all their knowledge and power could be passed on from one generation to the next. They made and used rattles—gourds or terrapin shells or skin dried over wooden frames and always decorated according to their purposes. They kept bundles of sacred objects, which must be re-newed and purified from time to time, for use in worship and in heal-ing. If they were not renewed, they lost their power. Since none of these things were written in books, every object and ceremony had to be studied and its use and meaning handed on without mistake and with full understanding of its purpose. A man had to spend time in meditation and keep his mind clear and his heart good, to do these things.

Our musical instruments—drums, rattles, and whistles—were all made by the men of the tribe. Our drums were different from those used by the school band at Darlington and by the Army band at the Fort. Those had been manufactured and shipped there, while ours were homemade. Hand drums, the kind used at many of our dances, were small and were made by stretching a skin over a frame and fastening thongs at the back so the drum could be held in one hand and struck with the other. Then we had our kettledrums, which were made by stretching a hardened skin over the top of a kettle or a pail, with water inside to make the tone deeper and more lasting. For many of our dances we used a round drum fixed to the ground by stakes, and so big that several drummers and singers could sit around it. Our whistles were made of eagle or wild turkey bones, hollowed out and notched in such a way as to make different whis-tling sounds. These, decorated with eagle breath feathers, were hung around the neck by a deerskin string, so that a warrior or a dancer could blow them at the right time in a ceremony. We had flutes, too, made of wood and notched in such a way that they made several notes, but these were used only by individuals and not in our ceremonies.

Fathers and mothers made fine toys for their children. For their little girls, Arapaho mothers made dolls dressed in perfect buckskin costumes, beaded and fringed just as our own costumes were. The tiny moccasins these dolls wore were made as carefully as moccasins for people, top sewed to bottom with deerskin string that came together in a kind of tassel at the heel. Such perfect little things made even a great chief smile, and pleased everyone that saw them. Often a little girl's mother made her a toy tipi, like a white child's playhouse, with a little bed and back-rests to go inside it. Sometimes the child had a little rack for drying meat outside, and a parfleche to hold her doll's clothing. Or she might have a tiny wooden horse for her doll to ride, with a travois dragging behind.

Fathers made bows and arrows for their sons, and made them so true that little boys could bring down squirrels or birds with them. Sometimes the boys dressed the squirrel they had shot, and cooked and ate it, and then sat around their fire telling their "buffalo story," as if they were old hunters. Often the father made his son a quiver for his arrows, and the little fellow learned to reach back over his shoulder with the same quick motion he had seen his father make. Nearly every small boy had a top made of cedar wood, and a two-tongued quirt to use in the game of whipping tops. Men made snowsnakes, too, out of polished buffalo ribs with two sticks tipped with eagle feathers wedged into the hollow of the bone and fastened there with sinews. Grown men, as well as boys, played snowsnakes, shooting them on snow or smooth ground over a little mound built up to give the snowsnake force.

To all of us, clothing was important. Styles did not change for us from year to year, as those of the white people did, for we had developed a way of dressing that suited the life we lived and the materials we had, and we saw no need to change it. When we came upon some item of clothing that we liked, after the traders came among us, we added that to our costume. Some of the young men, braves who thought a good deal about how they looked, bought little hand mirrors, mounted them in leather, and wore them dangling from their wrists as they danced. The mirror flashed in the light as the dancer moved, and he could look into it to renew his paint or smooth his hair, just as a woman renews her powder and lipstick from a little box in her purse today. We liked color and ornament and grace in our dress, and we thought most of the white people's clothing was dull and uninteresting. Our men draped their blankets over their shoulders or about their waists, as they needed them, and could throw them aside or drape them across their ponies' backs when they were riding, without any bother over buttons or sleeves. Beneath their blankets they might wear buckskin leggings and shirts of skin or cloth, with the tails hanging loose, as boys like to wear them today. A man could strip to a breechcloth and moccasins in no time and still, because of his brown skin and fine figure, not look bare or half dressed.

The women's finest costume was a fringed buckskin skirt, smoked or white, cut straight and long, and a straight buckskin jacket. These were trimmed in several ways: with rows of elks' teeth, with beaded or painted designs, or with strings of beads or jingles added to the fringe. Our women never wore feather headdresses, but their long braids, shining and smooth, and the strip of color painted in the center parting of the hair made them look well-groomed and trim. Later, full skirts and waists of calico took the place of buckskin clothing, and shawls were worn for decoration and for warmth. It took an Arapaho woman or man to carry a shawl or a blanket across the arm and drape it about the waist or the shoulders or even over the head, as it was needed, with real grace and without allowing it to slip out of place. White women of today do not manage their stoles so well.

When the weather was warm enough, and we Arapaho could stand a good deal of cold, little children ran about the camp without any clothing or with only a breechcloth and moccasins. Much of the time this was covering enough, though the white people at the Agency did not think so. They all believed in covering up as much of the body as possible. Today in summertime, when white people dress their children in sunsuits and sandals, letting their skin grow brown in the sun, they remind me of the way we looked in my childhood, running around among the tipis, tanned and free and naked, or nearly so.

As a schoolboy at Darlington and later on as an employee there, I remember the men and women busy about the camp and the children playing they were busy at the same tasks. Nobody seemed hurried or worried; nobody set a time when a thing had to be done, or complained of his tools or his materials. He had all the time the sun above gave him and all the materials Mother-Earth provided. There were no bosses and no employees, no wages and no strikes. What was made by our men and women then was beautiful and lasting, and more suited to our needs than anything we have bought in stores since we have followed the white man's road.

I have gone to the style show at the University of Oklahoma, where students display clothing they have designed and made. Some of the dresses and wraps and bags and scarves were made in color combinations and with designs in decoration taken from those of some of our Indian tribes. It pleased me to have Indian crafts given this recognition. But they gave little more than a hint of the labor and the skill that went into our clothing when every stitch was made by hand on robes that the women had dressed and tanned themselves, with tools of their own making.

5

From Fighters
to Freighters

WHEN WE FIRST SAT DOWN on the Reservation, the Agents and those who directed them in Washington expected all the Arapaho men to become farmers. There was plenty of rich land, and they expected each man to choose ground wherever he wanted it within our boundaries and settle down. But the Arapaho had always lived in bands, with their tipis side by side, their horses grazing together, and with hunting and fighting and feasting and worship all carried on by the group. It took years to learn to settle down on a farm and work alone and see one's neighbors only once in a while. Neither we nor our dogs nor our ponies understood this new way of the white people. To us it seemed unsociable and lonely, and not the way people were meant to live.

Even our tribal leaders, great men at hunting and fighting and conducting social gatherings and religious ceremonies, knew nothing about how to prepare ground or what seed to plant and when to plant it, or how to plant and cultivate and harvest and store the crops. Those of us who were boys and were taught farming and dairying in the schools had a better chance to learn than our fathers had. We could grow up with the new idea. But even we had some problems in our education as farmers, for the country was new to the Agents and the teachers and the other employees. Sometimes all the corn failed, because of heat and drought; sometimes grasshoppers and locusts swept in and ate up everything. After a few years, the Agents and the Agency farmers were ready to admit that cattle raising and dairying were better, on most of our land, than raising corn and oats.

Some of our boys and men were learning other things besides farming. Mr. Seger had built a brick plant, where some of the men of both of our tribes learned to mix and mold and fire brick. Once in a while, some fellow who was good at molding would challenge the others to a public contest, with a prize put up for the winner by the editor of the *Cheyenne Transporter* or by one of the traders. That made a good game out of a hard job, and was great sport. We had always had contests of skill and strength in the old days, and we enjoyed them. And we made good bricks. Some of the buildings still standing, on the old Agency grounds and at the Mennonite Mission, are built of them.

We learned to cut and store hay, too. We had always moved our horses from one place to another, summer and winter, for good grazing; now we learned to move the grass to the horses and to store it in stacks or in bales. This was new to us, but we saw how it worked. Our ponies no longer grew weak and lean in winter, when snow and ice covered the dried grass. If there were good rains, the prairies and the hay fields could be cut not once but several times during the season. It was something we could hardly believe. We saw that the men who taught us were smart, and had a new kind of power. Brinton Darlington himself had begun putting up hay on the Agency farm, and showing us how and why it should be done. He taught us to prepare for a hard winter every year, instead of hoping and making medicine for a mild one.

What astonished us more than anything else was learning that the white man cut and stored ice in winter, for use in summer. That was before he had gone still farther and invented machinery to make ice the year around, instead of storing it. At the Agency they built a thick-walled storage house, and when the ponds and streams were frozen solid they sawed the ice into blocks, hauled it in, and packed it in sawdust from the Agency sawmill. We had never heard of ice in summer before. It would have seemed like strong medicine, if we had not seen for ourselves how it was done. But when the next sum-

mer came, and some of the Indians drank the white man's iced lemonade, and when we tasted his ice cream, we knew that the white
man had more schemes for comfort and good living than we had
ever dreamed of.

Gradually, a good many of us, especially older boys and young
men, came to be employed at the Agency, if we had learned to do
some kind of work that was needed there. A few who had gone to
Hampton or Carlisle, or later to Haskell Institute, and were good at
the kind of learning that comes from books, interpreted for one tribe
or the other, or worked in the commissary or in the brickyard or at
the sawmill. I worked in the dairy at Darlington and later at other
Indian schools, for I liked livestock and I had learned from the
Mennonites in the mission school at Darlington and later at Halstead,
Kansas, how to feed and care for them. Now and then, for some of
the men not working regularly, there were jobs like cutting hay on
the prairie, or building and mending fences, or cutting firewood and
fence posts.

I have always been glad that as a boy and a young man I had
the kind of schooling I had. It brought me back to the Reservation
again, each time after I had been away, and gave me employment at
one place or another among my own people. When my school days
and my travels as a young man were over, I came to Rainy Mountain
to take charge of the livestock at that Government school. It was
there that I met Hattie Powless, an Oneida who was a matron there.
Like the Arapaho, the Oneida like to sing, and have many beautiful
songs. So we became friends, and later we were married. We never
had a permanent farm home of our own, or even a permanent home
in town somewhere, because we lived at whatever school or mission
employed me and where she, too, was sometimes employed as matron
or housekeeper. Our four children, three sons and one daughter,
though they were half Oneida, always thought of themselves as
Arapaho, or at least as Plains Indians, because it was among these
Indians that they grew up.

After we left Rainy Mountain we went to Saint Patrick's, the
Roman Catholic Mission near Anadarko. Father Isidore was in
charge there, and the children and the employees all liked him very

much. Sometimes, in the evenings, the Episcopal minister from the church at Anadarko would ride out for a visit with him. These two spent long evenings together, and one of the things they liked to talk about was horses and horse racing. That kind of talk was enough to please any Indian.

My wife came from the country around Green Bay, Wisconsin, and like most of the Indians there she was an Episcopalian. Years after we were married, we went back to visit her relatives at Green Bay. There were doctors and lawyers and businessmen among those Indians there, and I was proud of her people and of what they had accomplished, just as I am proud of the Arapaho. We went to the Episcopal church there, and the singing was fine. Since her death I have had no real home of my own, but I always find some place where I can live and paint and keep in touch with my family and my Indian and white friends.

All this was a long way from the buffalo road we had once traveled. But much of it was beyond us at first, and without training and time enough to learn to understand it we could not follow it. I have heard of groups of white people who have gone to Mexico or South America to take up a new road of their own and have failed in it and come back to their old homes to start over again. But we had no home to go back to; we could only follow the old road as long as it lasted, while we learned the direction of the new one.

Buffalo herds still roamed on the Reservation during our first few years there; and twice a year, as in the old free days, the Cheyenne set out on their buffalo hunt and we on ours. Both tribes held their buffalo dances before they set out, and got their bows and arrows and knives and guns ready for use. The women struck the tipis, packed the lodge poles and robes and kettles and parfleches on travoises drawn by the gentlest of our horses, and "went to buffalo." It was not an easy life, but it was a fine one: men, women, children, dogs, and horses moving together across land that had no roads or fences; temporary camps set up where grass was fresh and water plenty; hunting along the way, for deer and quail and turkey and prairie chicken and wild fruits and nuts to live on until they came to buffalo.

When a herd was sighted, the real action began. Men in breechcloths and moccasins jumped on their fastest, smartest horses, and all of them, circling and yelling, made the big surround. Heavy as they were, the buffalo were fast and hard to kill. When a herd was on the run, it was like thunder rolling over the ground too fast and furious to stop. If a man's horse stumbled, he might be trampled to death by the running herd. But the men could ride like the wind, and their horses, without the extra weight of a saddle and a man's heavy clothing, were as quick and smart as their riders. It was more of a game than football or polo is. It covered more ground and brought bigger results. Everything we were to have to eat and wear and shelter us for the next six months depended on it.

Every hunter, picking his buffalo, tried to circle in such a way as to send his arrow or his bullet just back of the buffalo's left shoulder, so as to reach his heart. But the hide was tough, and the animal was running and plunging and pawing, and the whole herd was running with him, getting into the hunter's way. Often the best a hunter could do was to send an arrow into the animal's hide, between the hump and the shoulder, crippling him. Then another arrow, or a bullet, could be sent to the heart. When the buffalo that had been shot were down and the rest of the herd had thundered away, the women and children moved in, and skinning and butchering and feasting began. It was the women who were busy then, while the men rested and ate and told stories of this and other hunting days.

We never killed more buffalo than we could use, to eat and to bring back in the form of hides and robes, dried meat and pemmican and tallow. So, we believed, the Indians and the buffalo would hold out together as long as grass grew. It was white men who slaughtered buffalo without limit, and brought our long-traveled buffalo road to an end. Some of them killed whole herds, for no reason except that they wanted to be rid of them. Men who built railroads and those who wanted to establish farms and towns had no use for them. A good many of these men had no use for Indians either, and the Indians and the buffalo were disappearing together.

The last of our hunts, before Reservation days began, were fights with white men as well. We hated the white men who slaughtered bulls and cows and calves alike and left them to rot on the prairies, and whenever we found them at it we attacked them. They had wagons and mules and camp gear to set up as barricades, and more ammunition than we had. But our horses were better trained than theirs, and we were better riders and sometimes better marksmen. Still, there were too many white men crossing the country to get to California, settling on the land to farm it, and building railroads and bridges. Each year the herds grew fewer and smaller, and our scouts went farther in search of them. By the time of the Medicine Lodge treaty, we had seen signs that the day had come when there would be no more buffalo. We wanted to believe what we had always believed, that the buffalo came up out of a hole in the ground somewhere out on the western Plains and that if we held our dances and used the buffalo as we had been taught to do, there would always be more. But our medicine was gradually losing its power.

After we came to the Reservation, we could not hunt beyond its boundaries. For a few years we still had good hunts, and came in with plenty of meat and robes and hides. The white people at the Agency thought we were irresponsible and lazy, when we left our gardens and field crops to go on the summer hunt, or when we took our children from school to go in winter time. But buffalo came first, in our minds, as long as any were left; we "went to buffalo" when buffalo were plenty, not when crops were laid by or schools dismissed. And since the promised Government issues of food and calico and lodge cloth were often delayed, so that we went cold and hungry while we waited, it is small wonder that, among the older people especially, the buffalo road seemed the one to follow. When I was growing up, old people on the Reservation still remembered those last buffalo hunts as the best thing they had ever known. Sometimes the Indians found white people within the Reservation boundaries, illegally shooting deer and antelope and turkey and prairie chickens, cutting our timber, stealing our horses and cattle. Even then we could not make war on the trespassers because we had pledged ourselves to peace, and the Agents reported that, considering the situation, the crimes we committed were very few. The last good buffalo hunt on the Reservation was in 1874. The next winter was very cold; the hunt was a failure; our lodge skins were worn out and our ponies thin for want of grazing; our annuity goods were long delayed; there was much sickness and hunger and death. Even the Cheyenne, most of whom had refused to send their children to school until then, began to see that they must take the new road. The old one had come to an end.

The white people at the Agency were learning something too. They were learning that we could not become farmers overnight because we were told to, and that we had strength and energy that must be used. Strong men, once horsemen and hunters and fighters, could not sit down in idleness without becoming sullen and discontented. Then Agent Miles, with some of our leaders, worked out a plan for the Cheyenne and the Arapaho to become freighters. There were no railroads to bring in what was needed at the Fort and the Agency to stock the traders' stores; there were no wagon roads that could properly be called roads. The freighting of goods and food from Kansas had always been a slow, hard, risky job, carried on by men driving teams of mules or oxen. The freighter had to be ready to stand all kinds of weather, summer or winter, eating camp food, fording rivers, fighting prairie fires. We Indians were used to bad weather and camp life, and we had hundreds of ponies that were idle. Mr. Miles believed that we could become freighters. Many white people understood us so little that they thought we would run away with the freight, or lose or damage it on the road, or use the time away from home to start an uprising. But we were honorable and responsible, and we hadn't lived by hunting and trading over the Great Plains for hundreds of years for nothing.

The trail the freighters followed could not be called a road. It was over the old Chisholm Trail for most of the way. This was a cattle trail, wide and dusty or muddy most of the time, and slow for wagon travel whenever cattle were being driven along it. About thirty miles of our route, from Darlington north to Dover, ran a few miles west of the Chisholm Trail and was known as the Traders' Trail. From Darlington, it was one hundred and ten miles to Caldwell, one hundred and thirty-five to Arkansas City, and one hundred and sixty-five to Wichita. These were the points in Kansas where freight for Darlington was loaded. Sometimes Arapaho made the trip and sometimes Cheyenne, but we never combined. Usually one of our village chiefs was in charge of a train, because he was a leader and knew the men under him. At least one member of the Indian police went along with each train, to act with the chief as leader and to be in authority when they reached the town where they picked up their loads. They were off the Reservation then, and someone in authority must be responsible for them. Sometimes there were only five or six teams to a train, and sometimes there were thirty or forty, depending on the amount of freight to be hauled. A train in ordinary weather could cover from twenty-five to thirty miles a day; but if there was mud or snow or trouble with wagons or horses or flooded streams to cross, no one could tell how long a trip might take. The Government furnished wagons and harness, until the men driving the teams had earned enough to pay for them; after that, each man owned his outfit. He had furnished his own horses from the beginning.

These horses knew how to race and turn on the track of a steer, or how to draw a travois on the march, but to most of them freighting was new. They had never hauled a wagon, and they didn't like harness. Four horses, hitched two and two, made a team; the two ahead were called leaders and the two behind were called wheelers. They were not guided by lines fastened to bridles, the way a white man's workhorses were; instead, the drivers rode on other horses at the sides of a team to guide them. By yelling and cracking their whips and pushing the horses along, they kept them going forward over the trail. Usually, too, the wives of the drivers went along, sitting on the wagon seat or in the wagon itself in their fine, bright clothes, yelling at the horses and visiting with one another as they moved along. Even the horses were decorated for the trip, with bright red or yellow or green cloth braided into their manes and tails. Altogether, it was a busy, noisy, good-natured undertaking, which everyone enjoyed because it was a little like the old marches when a village moved or a party went out to hunt, and because when the freight was brought safely in to Darlington or Fort Reno there was money to spend afterward.

Everybody went into action when there was a stream to ford. The horses hated to go down the slippery banks into the water, and a good deal of yelling and shoving was needed to keep them going and to bring them up the grade on the other side. If the river was in flood, the driver and the women and children as well as the horses had to swim; and if the horses balked at the high water, everybody yelled and whacked and pushed and pulled till they were in up to their shoulders and had to swim. The goods in the wagon bed, high up above the wheels, were almost never damaged by water, but they would have been if the drivers hadn't kept the horses under control and known just where to make the best crossing. Anybody that couldn't swim or handle frightened horses or camp in cold and rain until ice melted or floods went down, had no business on a freighting trip. But there were wonderful days and nights on the road, as well as bad ones; sometimes there was a fine supper of turkey or quail or deer or land terrapin around the campfire; and always there was the good feeling of being outdoors with the sun and the moon and the changing seasons and the woods and grass and streams.

Once, when I was a little boy, I went on a freighting trip with my father, who was one of the Arapaho police. This was a short trip that took a little less than four days, to Oklahoma City where there was then a railroad and where some of the goods once hauled from Kansas could now be shipped. I remember the canvas-covered wagons bumping along, and the men riding and visiting by the side of the wagons, and the women and children tumbled together inside. Even the prairies between Darlington and Oklahoma City looked big to me then, with the sun shining high overhead and the North Canadian River turning and winding like a wide green band through the country. I remember a spot near Banner where there were big trees for shade, and grass and water for our ponies, and wood for fire. We made our nooning there. On the return trip, when we had camped for the night by the side of the trail, a summer storm came up, with thunder and lightning and heavy rain. The horses were frightened and plunged around in their hobbles, and the men worked for hours tightening up the canvas covers on the wagons and shifting the goods around to keep them from getting wet. I was inside one of the wagons, lying on a big box, and I was as badly scared as the horses were. I lay quiet and kept my fears to myself, as any Indian boy knew how to do, but I thought what it must be like to go on a trip, two weeks or more, to Wichita and back, with wider rivers to ford and with no warm lodge walls to shelter me for many nights. Anyhow, we got our loads in to Darlington the next day after the storm, without any damage to any of the goods. It was fine to pull in to the Agency with ponies running, wagons creaking and swinging, drivers yelling, and everybody running out from buildings to hear the news of the trip. I never went with the freighters again, for by the time I was old enough to go as a driver the railroad had been built to El Reno and freighting was about over.

There were more than two hundred and fifty wagons hauling freight when the business was at its height. Sometimes, in a year of freighting, with over a million pounds hauled, there was a perfect record of no damage or loss. The pay was not much, a dollar a hundredweight. Divided among the heads of all the families that had had a part in the hauling, I suppose that might be considered very poor pay. But we needed less then than people need today, and money bought more. Even a penny bought something then. And besides, we weren't freighting just for the pay we got, but for some of the kind of satisfaction that we once got out of hunting and fighting. The Agents began to trust the Cheyenne and the Arapaho then, when they saw what we could do year after year as freighters. There was almost no drinking and gambling on those trips, though the white people in Kansas put plenty of chances for those things in our way. The influence of Little Raven, even after his death, was strong against drinking and gambling, and men like White Cloud had the same kind of influence among the Cheyenne.

Sometimes the freighters had a load both ways. Some of the Arapaho cut fence posts to haul up to Kansas to sell, for fencing was being done everywhere up there, and there was always a sale for posts. Sometimes the women took along handwork that they had done to sell—embroidered shirts and moccasins and children's toys.

Traders and travelers in Kansas had begun to ask for these things, and they sold well if we had an interpreter along to help us understand what kind of bargain we were making. Now and then, a group of Indian boys and girls on their way to school in Kansas or in the East, with interpreters and school matrons and parents, rode up in the wagons to some point where they could take the train. This was slower travel for them than by the Darlington stagecoach, but it was more sociable and there was no fare to pay.

Once in a while, we were cheated in what we bought or sold, and on a few trips some of our ponies were stolen while we were in town loading our wagons, but we got through without any fights. We kept out of trouble and we brought our freight in. We had given our word.

17. INDIAN WAR.

18. PRAYER BEFORE ENTERING THE TIPI FOR A PEYOTE CEREMONY.

19. Buffalo Hunters Skinning a Buffalo.

20. An Indian War.

21. A War Party Attacking.

22. A Peyote Ceremony.

Courtesy of Mrs. Gertrude Phillips.

6

Wohaw

We Arapaho had always been a sociable people. In our old way of life it had been necessary for us to live in bands, or villages of tipis, and to carry on all our important undertakings together; so we found it hard, in the early days on the Reservation, to learn to work and plan as individuals. Every occasion that brought us together gave us pleasure. We gathered for it early and wore the best we had and made the most of the chance to visit and feast and celebrate. So grass payments and annuity issues meant big times in our lives.

The grass money was rental for lands on our Reservation that we leased to white men for cattle grazing. Since nobody owned the land individually and there was far more of it than we could cultivate and farm, it was leased in large tracts in the name of the Cheyenne and the Arapaho tribes, through the Agent, and the money for the leases was paid to us once a year. Every man, woman, and child received an equal share. Often many of us had spent most of our money in advance, before it was paid to us, but all of us went to the Agency anyhow at the time of the grass payments. Sometimes we had spent our money wisely, for farm implements or household goods; sometimes we hardly knew where it had gone, for one thing or another at the commissary or at the store, where we had been given credit. But we made a good thing of the gathering. Even though the Agents tried to persuade us to come to the pay table wearing no paint and dressed in what they called civilized clothing, and even though many of us had little or no cash to take home with us when the traders had deducted what we owed them, we were all there and in a good mood. There was trading at the stores and feasting in the tipis and visiting everywhere, and everybody went away happy.

By the terms of the treaty at Medicine Lodge, the United States Government was to furnish us what we needed to live on, after we sat down on the Reservation, until we had time to learn to provide for ourselves. It was also to give us schools and teachers, and farm implements and blacksmiths and Agency farmers, to start us on the corn road. All this was paid for out of the fund credited to us for our claim to lands that we surrendered when we moved to the Reservation. Each winter, under this plan, we received an issue of what was called annuity goods. What we were given varied from year to year, but usually there were blankets, strouding for lodge covers, calico and denim for the women to use in making clothing, coats and trousers and shoes and stockings, axes and knives, and needles and thread and kettles and frying pans. Often the goods, which were supposed to reach us at the beginning of winter for use during the cold months ahead, were delayed a long time in the shipping; often, too, they had been carelessly packed and handled, so that the cloth was stained and mildewed and the knives and pans were rusty. And although the Agent and his men were good at figures, there was always some mistake in the count and not enough of any one thing for everyone. Sometimes there was a new lodge covering for only one family in three, or one pair of shoes for every two men. We laughed at some of these shortages and made the best of them. If a man's share of shoes was only one instead of a pair, that was reason enough for the men to sell their shoes and wear moccasins. And if only part of the men got trousers, that was a good excuse to cut them up and wear them as leggings, as the older men usually wore them anyhow.

Each Agent distributed the goods according to his own system, but usually he portioned out whatever we were to get among the village chiefs, to be divided as they thought best. They were responsible men and knew the needs of each family, and they almost never failed to make a fair distribution as far as the goods went. Often we were disappointed over what Washington sent us, but I never heard of any quarrels between Indians over the issue, even when there was far too little to go around and the need was great.

Sometimes the Agents threatened to withhold the annuity goods, to compel us to send our children to school or to give up our medicine dances or to break sod and plant crops. They even threatened to withhold the goods from families of men who refused to cut their hair and to wear trousers. But there was nothing in the terms of the Medicine Lodge treaty to permit this kind of withholding, and the Agents learned not to try it. It made us sullen and uncooperative, and turned us back toward the old road rather than forward to the new.

Wherever we lived on the Reservation—and as the years went on, some of our villages were as much as sixty-five miles away—everyone that could make the trip was on hand at the Agency for the annuity issue. Many of the people, coming from a distance, brought their tipis and camping equipment with them and settled down at Darlington to visit and enjoy life together until the distribution was over. They walked or rode on ponies with a travois dragging behind or came in wagons, and a few of them rode in carriages. The Agents and the teachers argued against an Indian's buying a carriage when he needed, they said, to buy a stove and beds and chairs and farm equipment, but the Indian who managed to get together enough money to buy a carriage argued that he had been told to try to do as the white people did, and white people rode in carriages. We couldn't do everything at once; so we did first what pleased us most.

All of us wore our best to the Agency for the annuity issue. The women came dressed in their buckskin jackets and leggings, or in calico dresses with bright shawls or blankets over them; they carried their babies on cradle boards and led along small children wearing beaded buckskin or calico or denim, with small shawls and blankets of their own. The men with long hair oiled their braids and bound them with otter skin or with colored string, and wore hats on top of these, if they had hats. There was every color and every kind of clothing to be seen, and everyone was in good spirits. Annuity meant a happy, sociable time for everyone. The children played such Indian games as the hoop-and-stick and the mud-ball game, or prisoner's base and drop-the-handkerchief that they had

learned from white children; the young men raced their ponies up
and down the Agency streets, showing off; the older people, who
hadn't seen one another in a long time, sat together for hours in
the lodges, visiting and telling stories of the old days. Hunting
stories, war stories, stories of brave marches and hard winters and
perfect summers when the buffalo grew fat and the bushes were
loaded with wild fruit, were told over by those who remembered
them. All around the Agency, for two or three miles up and down
the river, the tipis glowed at night from the center fires inside.

When the goods were distributed, everyone put on something
new—a blanket or a hat or a coat or a shirt or a shawl. If a man got
a pair of shoes or trousers that he did not want, he sold them or
traded them off for something he fancied for himself or his family.
There was trading going on everywhere, and those who came out
of a deal with something to sell or with some money to spend now
went to the traders' stores to see what they could get. We were
always glad to have coffee and sugar and flour, and maybe some
canned goods, to take home with us. By the time the gathering broke
up, everyone had something new and everyone was happy.

Food was issued on a different plan. At first when we raised no
crops and had no knowledge of how to do any kind of work that
would give us employment at the Agency, nearly all of our food had
to be issued to us. Beef was issued only after we no longer had
buffalo meat or when smaller game was not to be had. Every two
weeks other items of food that white people considered necessary to
live on were distributed to us: bacon and salt pork, flour, sugar, salt,
coffee, and lard. Some of these things, especially the bacon and the
salt pork, we had to learn to eat, because they were too salty for our
taste. Later, when the buffalo were all gone and even small game
was less plentiful, but when many of us began to have foodstuffs
from our farms and some money to buy part of our supplies, only
beef and flour were issued. These rations were supposed to be enough
to last each family for two weeks, but it was hard for any Indian
to learn to divide what he had on hand and make it last fourteen
days. It had always been our custom to feast when food was plenty
and to share all we had when there were visitors. We had our own

laws of hospitality and our own faith that the powers we prayed to
would provide for us. The advice our Agents gave us to cut wood
in summer when it was hot to use in winter when it would be cold,
to stack hay before frost, to dry corn and beans and save sugar and
flour for the future was hard for us to follow. The Agents thought
we were wasteful and blind to everything but the present, but they
had never grown up in a village that used and enjoyed whatever
food and fuel and pasture was at hand and then moved on to where
there was sure to be more.

Among the Arapaho, and many other Indians, the word for
beef was "wohaw." This was not an Indian word, in the old sense.
We had never seen cattle until we saw white men driving their ox
teams across the country. The driver had a good deal of whacking
and yelling to do to keep them going, and "Wo!" and "Haw!" were
what he yelled at them. So, having no word for the oxen in our
language, we called them wohaw. When we slaughtered a beef and
ate it, we called that wohaw too.

Our older people had to learn to like wohaw. Meat had always
been their principal food, and whatever else they had they were
always hungry without it. But beef had a different smell and a different taste from buffalo; it was stronger and not so sweet. And since
the contractors who supplied the beef bought range cattle, often thin
and of poor grade, for the commissary, the meat was likely to be
tough. It took long cooking to make a range steer tender, and we
had always eaten our buffalo meat rare. But we children who had
been born on the Reservation liked the white man's meats, beef and
bacon and salt pork, from the beginning.

Mondays were beef-issue days, wohaw days. At first the beeves
were all issued by the Government clerk from one station, the big
corral across the river from the Agency, southeast of Fort Reno. This
meant that every two weeks some member of a family had to be on
hand to get his beef, and for those families living at a distance from
the Agency this meant a long trip, breaking into whatever work
was being done at home. So ten stations were set up at different
points on the Reservation, with a blacksmith's shop there for repair-
ing farm tools and shoeing horses, a white farmer whose work was

to teach the Indians around him how to farm and to care for livestock, and a corral for the beef cattle that were to be issued. After
that, nobody had more than a few miles to go.

Issue days were big times for all of us. The men who were to
do the killing painted their faces and rode their fastest horses and
brought along their best bows and arrows, or their guns. The women
followed along, usually with a pony travois to carry the smallest
children and to bring home the beef. People all put on some of their
finery, and braided some colored cloth into the manes and tails of
their horses, and made a holiday out of the work they had to do.
All across the prairies, on Monday mornings, people in bright colors
and high spirits came riding to the issue station. There were visiting
and excitement and work and feasting ahead for everyone. One by
one, as the clerk stamped the ration tickets of the heads of families,
the men in the corral drove a beef from the pen and sent it down
the chute. Yelling and racing his pony and with his family coming
along behind as close as they could manage to do, the man rode
after his wohaw as it bellowed and plunged and tore across the
prairie, trying to escape. Wohaw could run almost as fast and bellow
and turn almost as wildly as the buffalo once did. For a few hours,
the Arapaho knew once more some of the excitement of the old
buffalo hunt. And when at last the beef was shot down, the women
moved in with their knives and kettles, skinning the hide off and
cutting up the meat to take back to their lodges. Everybody had a
piece of the raw liver, fresh and warm, before the families set out
for home. Then, in the tipis or outside, fires were kindled; some of
the beef was cooked, and the feasting began. Lodge walls were lifted
at the sides if the weather was good, and the skins at the entrance
were propped up overhead, so that several lodges could be thrown
together during the feast. It was a time of plenty and of hospitality
for everyone.

Next day the women were busy outside the tipi, cutting into
strips whatever meat was left and hanging it from poles to dry. We
had never heard of refrigerators in those days, but the sun and the
wind soon cured the meat so that it did not spoil. The cattlemen who
leased pastures on our Reservation called this jerked meat, or jerky.

But usually there was little left of our wohaw for drying. When there was anything to feast on in our villages, we feasted well.

After 1896, the method of issuing beef was changed. To shorten the time required for the issue, and to do away with the celebrating that went with it, live beeves were no longer given out. Instead, the cattle were slaughtered, and issued from the block. At first all the men objected to the change, and the chiefs protested to the Agent. Many a Cheyenne family went hungry until the proud chiefs of that tribe decided they must bow to authority and accept slaughtered beef. The sport that had been as important as the feasting on issue days was ended with that change from beef on the hoof to beef on the block. Progress was catching up with us.

7

Teachers, Travelers, Preachers

EVEN NOW when I am old and have known a great many people, I believe the best and finest of them all were those I knew at Darlington. There was, of course, John Seger, who came among the first and stayed the longest and was probably known to every Cheyenne and Arapaho on the Reservation. It was on Christmas Eve in 1872 when he arrived at the Agency to help put up the new buildings. After that first Christmas among us, he was always in demand, with his jokes and his tricks, to act as Santa Claus at all the different Christmas parties there, for the schools and for the Agency employees. Between the time when he came and the end of our Reservation days, he had almost every kind of job there—builder, farmer, stageline operator, and teacher—and he was even acting Agent for a while. Always he was someone from whom we could learn. He was so quick at knowing when the Indian boys were up to some kind of mischief that many of them believed he had some kind of power or medicine that the rest of the white people did not have. Once, when some Arapaho schoolboys let their appetites get ahead of their discipline, they planned to break into the bakery and have one of the boys hand out cookies and pies and cakes to the others outside below the window. But Mr. Seger, who had heard them talking and knew what they said in Arapaho, stood below the window and took the good things to eat as they were handed out to him. So the boys got no pies and plenty of punishment.

He rigged up an old magic lantern that someone had given him, and entertained everyone with talks and pictures in the evenings; he got friends from outside to send magazines and newspapers and books, which he used in the schoolroom to make the Indian children realize that reading was something more than a hard chore and was a means of finding out what was going on in the world. He introduced all sorts of games, from jackstraws to tugs of war, while he was at Darlington, for he knew that children, boys especially, needed plenty to do to keep out of mischief. He liked singing and other kinds of music, and when he found that the Indians could learn the white man's kind of music as well as their own, he got hold of some song books and taught the children to sing American songs. He thought that games and songs would help us to learn to use English and like it, as studying it only in books would not do, and in this he was right. We had to think fast when we were playing games or singing, and we could not take time to remember how the words looked in our reading and spelling books. We had to be able to say them, fast.

Most of all, Mr. Seger was a planter and farmer. The fine old trees still standing at Darlington are some of the many he planted there. In 1886 he took a band of Arapaho and another of Cheyenne with him to a new location about sixty miles southwest of the Agency, which was called Seger's Colony and later became the town of Colony, Oklahoma. Here where there was fine farm land and nothing to disturb them or lure them away from work, these Indians settled in camps and chose land for their farms. Mr. Seger himself ran the plough to prepare the fields for the first planting, and half a dozen Indian boys followed behind, dropping corn in the furrows. Here again he got a stock of young trees to plant; there are Indians living today who can remember carrying in their arms the little sprigs that are now great shade trees in the Colony neighborhood. They can remember Mr. Seger's children, who spoke Arapaho like the little boys and girls they went to school with, and Mrs. Seger who helped the women learn to cook and sew and who rode the neighborhood on horseback to make sure that no fences were down around the fields. The whole family was an example to us all. Some people said that Mr. Seger couldn't spell any better than the Arapaho could, but we were more in need of other things than we were of a good speller among us. At least most of us thought so. We liked him so much that we gave him an Arapaho name, "Neatha," which means "White Man." And he liked us so much that he in turn named one of his sons Neatha Seger. Neatha is still living, at Geary in the old Arapaho country, and can tell many a good story about how he grew up among us.

After the Quaker agents, whom we understood because they were patient and kind and held religious beliefs that did not interfere with our own, men came who did not understand us so well as Brinton Darlington and John Miles had done. Every time a few braves rode through the Agency streets wearing paint and dance costumes, these newcomers misunderstood what was happening and feared an uprising. They did not realize that we continued to hold our war dances for the sake of the old days, and to renew and strengthen our spirits. It was part of our religion and our tradition. Once, when a group of Cheyenne in paint and feathers galloped down the street at Darlington, giving their war whoops, the Agent, W. B. Dyer, was scared out of his senses. Those who knew what was going on tried to explain that these Cheyenne were only organizing a meeting of their Dog Soldiers. He spread the alarm among all the white people, and the more frightened he became the more our numbers increased in his mind. He sent word to Washington that at least a thousand soldiers would be necessary to protect the Agency from the great danger of an uprising of at least six thousand wild Indians. The troops that came from Kansas on a forced march must have been surprised at the peace and order they found at Darlington. Everybody laughed a good deal at this, and we wondered how Agent Dyer could have supposed we had forgotten our promise to keep the peace. After that, the Indian Commissioner usually appointed Army officers to act as Agents, men who had had experience among the Indians of the Plains and knew what the real signs of war were. These men were not frightened by the sight of a painted Indian or a war lance.

Most of these Army officers were fine men; they showed a good deal of authority and management, and they were as courteous in dealing with us as we tried to be with them. Sometimes, when they tried to withhold our rations or grass money to compel us to send our children to school or to wear what they called civilized dress, they were unpopular for a while. But we never lacked leaders to go to the Agent to explain how we felt about our ceremonies and dress and about enforced schooling, which for many years the Cheyenne especially opposed, and when the Agent understood our views we could reason with him. The first of these Army Agents that I can remember, when I was a little boy, was Captain Lee. He was here at the time when all white people leasing pasture lands from the Indians were required to take down their fences and leave, so that we could choose our own farm lands and settle down on them. White people predicted trouble with the Indians over that ruling, and said we would be sullen and unruly when our grass money was cut off. But Captain Lee kept a cool head and a firm hand, and there was no disorder. He gave the Arapaho credit for patience and cooperation, and he never favored a white man, in any dispute on the Reservation, just because he was a white man. When white intruders stole wood or livestock from us, he was willing to accept the evidence and see that they were punished. Whenever he could, he saw to it that the Indians got freighting contracts and the jobs of wood-cutting, fencing, clerking, and handling goods at the commissary. It was our Agency, he said, and he wanted us to prosper there.

I well remember Major Woodson, who came in 1893, the year after we had agreed to accept allotments of land and sell the rest of our Reservation to the government for white settlement. Many of us were still blanket Indians then, but we had accepted the duties of citizenship, and white families were beginning to move in among us. With these strangers and newcomers around us, many of them in need of cattle and horses and hogs to stock their farms, there was much stealing of our livestock, and many of our white neighbors who were too honest to steal were unfriendly because they were afraid of us. Probably it was because of Major Woodson, who was fair in all his dealings and understood how hard our situation was, that we got through without any disorder or bloodshed. Our record, he said, was better than that of the white citizens around us. But he had helped to make that record. Even I, a boy just home from school in Kansas when I first saw him, felt free to talk with him, and all the Indians knew him as their friend.

For many years during my childhood there was a hotel on the Agency grounds. It was run by a white man named John Murphy, and it had the reputation of being the best hotel along the stage route between Caldwell, Kansas, and Fort Eliott, Texas. The beds and the meals were so good that travelers making a long trip often stayed there an extra day or two, to rest and break their journey, while they saw the sights around the Agency and visited the traders' stores. On such days as Thanksgiving and Christmas, special meals were served there that were the talk of all the travelers that had to celebrate these holidays away from home. Mr. Murphy had a big cattle corral there, and good stables for travelers' horses. Sometimes ranchmen from as far away as Corpus Christi stayed there, on their way to or from the North where they sold their cattle. They could count on getting what they wanted at the Darlington Hotel, whether it was baled hay for their horses or iced lemonade and ice cream in the dining room on hot summer days. The Indians, as well as the white people, liked John Murphy. If any of them who had taken up farming had melons or sweet corn or berries to sell, he bought them for the dining table, paying them good prices in cash. After some years he sold the hotel to an Arapaho named Sitting Bull. But soon the town of El Reno grew up with two railroads there, so that the old stage-coach service and the old freighting were done away with. Then the Darlington Hotel was closed.

Once when I was a young man, a writer named Hamlin Garland came to visit at the Agency. He was a friend of Major Stouch, our Agent at that time, and he and Mrs. Garland rode all over the Reservation with Major and Mrs. Stouch. He had known Sioux and Arapaho and Cheyenne when he was a boy and was a great friend of all of them, hoping through the stories he wrote about them to make people everywhere understand them better. One of the things he wanted to improve for us was our system of names. He liked the names of the Cheyenne and the Arapaho, and he had reason to like them, for our names had meaning. People in our tribes named their children for some old member of the tribe, living or dead, who had shown some fine trait or done some fine deed, or for something in nature that they admired. That is why our women are called by such names as Grass Singing (Waanibe) and Singing Woman (Hisenibe), and our men by such names as Little Raven (Hohakaki) and Row of Lodges (Wanakayi) and Yellow Horse (Nihanisabad). These were given names, and there was nothing about them to show what family the person belonged to, as white people's names do. Also, when a man or woman had done something outstanding, he might be given a new name at our medicine ceremony, to show what he had done, or in memory of some man or woman who had once been great in the same way. We had no system of Christian, or given, names combined with family names. My father's name was Big Man and mine was Black; so there was nothing about my name to show that I was his son. When my older brother went to school at Halstead he took the name of the station Agent there, Fieldie Sweezy. Then when I entered school I was given the name Carl Sweezy, and all the children in our family took the same family name.

Now that we were taking up the ways of white people, and had been made citizens, Mr. Garland thought it was important that we follow the white man's system of names. Since we were taking individual farms and would hold and inherit land titles and other property, he thought we should have family names that would show our relationship. Also, he said that while many of our names had real meaning and beauty in our own language, they were translated so poorly that they became ugly or ridiculous in English. He was a friend of President Theodore Roosevelt, and both he and the President wanted to help us in this problem. But no rule was ever made about it, and even today there is sometimes confusion about how the members of our families are related. The children who went to school chose names for themselves, or their teachers assigned them names, and some of us today are known by two names, one white and one Indian.

The visitor whom I remember best of all, and who meant more to me than any outsider that came there, was James Mooney. He came many times from the Smithsonian Institution in Washington to study the ways and the beliefs of the Plains Indians, just as he had already studied those of some other tribes. It was hard for us to realize, when he first came, that there were now people employed by the Government who believed that our art and history and religion had value, and that instead of stamping out everything Indian they must do what they could to understand and collect and record everything that belonged to our way of living. This came as a big surprise. But nobody ever doubted Mr. Mooney's purpose for long, or felt that he spoke with a double tongue as some white people had been known to do. We believed that he respected what we were and did, even though we were different from him. He made us feel pride in the peculiar ways and dress and beliefs of the Cheyenne and the Arapaho. We gave him an Indian name, "Heniait," which means Long Hair, because when he was with us he wore his hair longer than other white men did.

Mr. Mooney came to what is now Oklahoma many times between 1891 and 1918. Sometimes he stayed with the Kiowas and the Apaches, and sometimes with us; sometimes he stayed with the Agency and sometimes with people out on the Reservation. We never knew when or where he might turn up, but we were always glad to see Long Hair. His longest visit must have been during the year 1895, when he stayed several months. Since the Darlington Hotel was closed then, and he needed a great deal of space where he could see his visitors and store the things he was collecting, he took up his quarters there. He had his wife and little son with him, and entertained many Indian visitors, especially old men and women who could answer his questions about the way things used to be. They brought old handwork and utensils with them, and shields and lances and bows and arrows and drums that he wanted to see. He hired Paul Boynton, the smart Cheyenne who had come back to the

Reservation after going to school at Carlisle, to act as his interpreter for the people from both tribes.

I was a boy of fourteen that summer, just back from the Mennonite school in Kansas where I had been for five or six years. I had brought back a baseball bat and a catcher's mitt, and had no idea of what I was going to do next except to teach some of the Indian boys around the Agency to play baseball instead of snow-snakes. I had been trying to draw ever since I was a little fellow, and a woman at the Agency had showed me how to use water colors. When Mr. Mooney said he wanted an artist to draw some of the designs on the handwork that was brought in and to restore the paint on some of the old shields that had been dug up, I was the best they could offer him. I sat nearby while he talked with the Indians about the shields and robes and leggings they brought in. Then I went to the room that Mr. Mooney had given me in the hotel and went to work. The next day, before the talks began again, I had made copies of what we had been looking at the day before. Mr. Mooney laughed and seemed surprised when I showed him the first one of these pictures, and praised it because the colors were true and the design was exactly like the original. So I worked for him as long as he stayed at the Agency, and after he left I kept on drawing and painting whenever I had the time and the materials.

Mr. Mooney was the only art teacher I ever had. When he left Darlington at the end of that stay he gave me some advice: Keep on painting, and don't paint rocks and trees and things that aren't there. Just paint Indian. So I am still painting, and painting Indian. It is the only way I know. I call it the Mooney way.

When he had finished his collection, Mr. Mooney gave a big party for everyone, white people and Indians. He called it an open house, and he held it in the big hotel rooms, with everything on display that he had collected there. He had everything, from a full-sized tipi to small rattles and charms, from cooking vessels to sacred bundles. He explained that he was now getting ready to pack all these things and ship them to the Smithsonian Institution in Washington, where they would never be lost or destroyed and where everyone that came to visit could see what we had accomplished and

how we had lived. Some of the old men and women there had made
the shields and lances and robes and moccasins that were on display
and were proud of their handiwork; all of us had proof that the old
road of the Arapaho had been a good one in its day and would not
be forgotten.

Teachers came and went, in the schools on the Reservation. At
first the Government schools were small and the attendance was
poor, for schools were a new idea to us. Parents and grandparents
and medicine men had always taught the children in the camps; we
had never heard of a teacher whose only work was to teach. Since
the Cheyenne had insisted on separate schools for their children,
there were always two Government schools at the Agency. Besides
these, there was the Mennonite Mission at Darlington, and later
there were other mission schools at other places on the Reservation.
Since my mother had died when I was quite small, I was taken in
at the Mennonite school at Darlington, which was in the charge of
the Reverend S. S. Haury. The first building put up by the Mennonites had burned, and the Haurys' baby and two small Indian
children had died in the fire. But this had not turned them back.
They had replaced the first building with a fine new one of brick,
three stories high and with a basement, a laundry nearby and a
garden and an orchard to furnish some of the food. This building
is still standing, empty now and out of repair, a little to the north
and east of the old Agency. I was proud to live in that building, that
stood up fine and tall on the prairie and could be seen for miles
away.

The Mennonites were of German descent, and were thorough
and orderly and systematic about everything they did. And they were
religious in a way that we Indian children could understand. From
the beginning, I remember the prayers and the Bible reading that
we had every morning and evening, and the songs we sang. Christian kindness was the spirit of the place. But while they were kind,
they were never lax or careless, and they never allowed us to be.
Even the smallest of us children began to learn to do things, indoors
and out, as well as to read and write and figure. We watched the
Mission people plough and harrow the soil in the garden, and when

it was ready for planting we helped put in the seeds—radishes and lettuce and onions close together in long rows, and melons and cucumbers and pumpkins in hills, far apart. After the seeds came up, we helped with the hoeing, and we learned what plants were crops, and what were weeds and how to pull them. We Arapaho children were close enough to our Mother-Earth to understand these things and to know that they were important. We never said we were tired and didn't want to pull weeds any more.

I remember that I was still a little boy wearing knee pants when the Mennonites sent me up to Halstead to their school there. It was probably because my older brother Fieldie was already there that they sent me, young as I was, and that I managed to fit in with the others. I began to learn dairying and the care of livestock, along with more things out of books, and my training was so thorough that for years afterward I was able to earn my living and a living for my family after I married, in one or another of the Government schools for Indians or at some one of the Indian missions.

Some of the Mennonites spoke German and sang German songs and hymns. Some of the Indian students there, good at books and at languages, learned to talk German and to read and write German script. For fun, they sometimes sent letters in that language back to people on the Reservation. Any letter, to an Indian on the Reservation, was something important, but a letter in German was something to talk about for a long time. To be able to write it was an accomplishment for a Cheyenne or an Arapaho, who had already learned, besides his own language, to talk in the sign language and to read and write in English.

When I was a young man, after I had been back from Halstead for a year or two, I was sent to school at Carlisle, in Pennsylvania, to go on with what I had been learning earlier from the Mennonites. That part of the country was different from what I had known on the Reservation and in Kansas; there were mountains there, and big rivers with rocky banks, and no prairies where we could see for miles in every direction. But we had good teachers there, and Captain Pratt, who was in charge of the school, believed that if Indians had a chance they could learn anything that white people could

learn. In the summer, those of us who were interested in farming
and dairying could be assigned to what was called a summer home.
For two summers I lived with a farmer's family at Washington Crossing, New Jersey, close to the Delaware River. Farming was not the
same there as it was on the prairies; the crops and the time of planting and harvesting were different. But I learned about their ways
too, and I liked to take care of the livestock I was put in charge of.
Those farmers around Washington Crossing had never believed that
an Arapaho was going to scalp them, but they were surprised that
I could be trusted with the full care of all the livestock on a farm.

I would have liked to stay at Carlisle until I could graduate.
But the winters were cold and damp there, and different from what
I had always known; and after two years I grew sick and was sent
back to the Reservation to get well. It was good to come back to
Darlington once more, to hear Arapaho spoken and take part in
Arapaho ceremonies and eat Arapaho food.

When I was well again, I was sent back to school, but not so
far away this time. I went to Chilocco Indian School, in the northern part of what was then Oklahoma Territory. On my way back
to Darlington at the end of that school year, when I changed trains
at Enid, I met one of my old school friends in the railway station.
He had signed up to play baseball with the Enid team and he thought
I was a good enough player to sign up too. We went to see some
of the men who were in charge of the business, and the next thing
I knew I was engaged to play all that summer. It was something I
had never expected to do, to enjoy playing baseball every day and
to be paid a salary for doing it.

Two of the young businessmen connected with the Enid baseball team were Frank and Orville Frantz. Frank had served as a
captain with Theodore Roosevelt's Rough Riders, and Roosevelt
thought highly of him just as everybody in Enid did. While Roosevelt was President, he appointed Frank Frantz to be Governor of
Oklahoma Territory. Years later I went back to Enid to see some
of the men I had known there, and had a fine visit with Frank and
Orville Frantz. We were still good friends.

A few years after the Mennonites began their mission at Darlington, Mr. Haury extended their work by opening a branch mission at Cantonment, sixty-five miles to the northwest of Darlington, for the children of the Arapaho that were settling down on farms there. Another Mennonite missionary, H. R. Voth, came with his family to take charge of the Darlington mission, and he and his wife were as faithful and as much interested in the school as the Haurys had been. Mr. Voth made a large collection of our handcrafts and equipment, and I am told that some of these things are still to be seen in the display at the Smithsonian Institution.

What the Mennonites accomplished as preachers and teachers can hardly be told. Because of their influence, many of the Arapaho today are members of the Mennonite Church. Through their teaching, many of our boys and girls grew up to be fine farmers and stockmen and housewives. When the missions on the Reservation were discontinued, in 1901, they had laid the foundation for the kind of life we were to live when our tribal days were over. We still try to live with principles of goodness and honor and faithful work, even though most of us living today know little of the white people who came in the early days to teach us these things.

Germans and Americans and Indians, traders and farmers and soldiers and anthropologists, Quakers and Episcopalians and Mennonites and believers in the religion of the Indian, we were all mixed up together there at Darlington. We Arapaho learned something from them all, and kept the best of our own beliefs as well. And it is to the credit of those who sat down with us on our Reservation, for a short time or a long one, that in the end we learned to follow the white man's road and became good American citizens.

8

Religion

WE ARAPAHO HAVE ALWAYS been a religious people. We had never built churches and held regular services in them, as white people did, and we had no book of sacred writings like the Bible, no prayer books and no hymnals. We had no fixed holy days and no Sabbath, no Thanksgiving Day feast and no Christmas. And when we first learned about Christmas, some of our children got the Baby Jesus and Santa Claus confused in their minds. For these reasons, it was hard for white people who lived among us to realize how important our religion was to us; it was hard for them to understand that everything we owned and every act of our lives was in some way connected with our religion.

All creation had a place in our religious beliefs. We believed in a power that was higher than all people and all the created world, and we called this power the Man-Above. We believed in some power in the world that governed everything that grew, and we called this power Mother-Earth. We believed in the power of the Sun, of the Night-Sun or Moon, of the Morning Star, and of the Four Old Men who direct the winds and the rains and the seasons and give us the breath of life. We believed that everything created is holy and has some part in the power that is over all. Some animals, such as the bear, the buffalo, and the badger, have more power than others. We have always known that the wild turkey has special power, and that the meadow lark understands and speaks Arapaho. Some plants, too, have the same kind of importance to us, such as the sweet-smelling cedar and the purifying sage. Such things were

made for us in the beginning; that is why we have always used them
in our ceremonies, being grateful for them and believing that they
would always grow where we could find them. Their power and
usefulness were for everyone. But certain things had power for particular persons. A man might go out to the hills or away on the
prairie alone, to fast and meditate and pray until he saw a vision or
fell asleep and had a dream that showed him what his own special
power and protection was. In his vision, a bird such as the eagle
or an animal such as the deer or the otter might talk with him, showing him some event that was to happen or something that he must
do for his family or his people. Always afterward this bird or animal
would give him success in his undertakings and protection when he
was sick or in danger. So he painted its picture on his shield or his
tipi wall, and he placed its feathers or its claws in his bundle of
sacred objects. He prayed to it when he needed help, and it did not
fail him. In the same way, a white man prays to God for help or
for knowledge about what he should do when he is undecided.

Sometimes a color or a design represented a man's power. Then
he painted himself with it and used it on his clothing and his arrows
and his horse. But he did not learn his protection and power easily;
he had to fast and pray and sacrifice before he learned it. And he
had to keep it alive in his mind and heart. If he became lazy or
careless and gave little attention to these matters, he might lose his
power.

Some men among the Arapaho, and among other Indians, had
special gifts. These were our priests and medicine men. They knew,
each one of them, everything connected with some one of our ceremonies; they knew songs and rituals for healing the sick and for
bringing success in war and hunting, for bringing rain, and for
warding off storms. They performed these services for anyone in
need of them, or for a whole village, and sometimes for the whole
tribe. They got their songs from older medicine men and priests, or
from visions of their own, and they had to have unusual gifts of
memory and understanding to do what they did. Some medicine
men had wives that shared the work of the ceremonies, especially
the singing; others did all their work alone. I have known medicine

men to foretell the arrival of visitors or the coming of storms or the approach of enemies.

Some medicine men had the special power of tipi-shaking. Such a man, bound and placed inside a small tipi within a lodge, sang until he called up the spirits that could answer what he wanted to know. When the voices of the spirits were heard talking to him, the tipi shook as if a high wind were blowing and the lodge poles creaked. After that, the thongs that had bound him were found to be untied. Then he could tell where a lost child was or, in the old days, where buffalo were and what enemy was approaching. White people, as well as Indians, have seen this ceremony performed and called it too strange and wonderful to be explained.

Once when I was visiting among the Osages, I got very sick with influenza. The white doctor could not cure me and I thought I might die. But the Osage medicine man performed his ceremonies for me, and boiled herbs in water, which I drank. The next day, although I was still weak, I was well again. I have known white doctors and ministers who have special knowledge and power, and do remarkable things for the bodies and the minds of people who need their help. The work of these healers and seers is part of some overall power too great to be understood by any one people or group. No one can see more than some part of its wonder. That is why there are so many religions.

Almost every act and custom among the Arapaho was part of their religion. The placing of our lodges in a circle open to the east, and the opening of each lodge on the eastern side, was religious. A man saw dawn when he woke, and prayed to the Man-Above and to Grandfather Sun and to the Four Old Men. He was thankful for the new day, and for the grass and the stream and the game that were outside his tipi. He was thankful for his strength and for his family, and for his village and his tribe. He did not eat food until he had made an offering to the Man-Above. If he had been unfortunate or had done some wrong, he purified his clothing and his weapons in the incense of cedar or sage that his wife had laid on the fire. These religious acts gave a man confidence and strength;

they made him a good fighter and a good hunter, and a good farmer after he began to follow the corn road.

It has always puzzled me to understand why people of one religious faith try to downgrade other faiths. Since I knew the Arapaho religion was good and true, I wondered why some Christians tried to undermine everything about it. Once, when there was an exhibit of Indian paintings on display in the Gilcrease Museum, Tom Gilcrease asked me to come and stay in the exhibit room to explain the paintings to anyone that asked about them. Tom was a Creek Indian, and he wanted everyone to understand more about all the Indian people. A Christian minister, one that I knew to be opposed to everything we Indians believed and to be outspoken about it, took a seat in the room near my painting of an Arapaho Sun Dance lodge. He explained to everyone who came by that the Sun Dance was heathenish and included such tortures that the dancers often died from them. I was mad enough to fight him, but the museum was not the place for a fight. Instead, I went over and sat down near him. I stayed right there. After that, nothing more was said about heathen Indians and cruel torture.

We had a good deal more understanding of the white man's religion than he had of ours. The Plains Indians had always done a good deal of tribal visiting with one another, and we knew that the songs and ceremonies of one tribe were different from those of other tribes. We respected them all, even though our own were the only ones we understood fully. But the white man wanted us to adopt the Christian religion, and to go to church on Sunday. Some missionaries wanted us to be Baptists or Mennonites or Methodists; others wanted us to be Episcopalians or Catholics. Nearly all of them wanted us to throw away our old religion. The Agents, speaking for the President in Washington, also wanted us to throw it away. They said it took too much of our time and made us neglect our crops and our livestock, and kept our children from school. But we could not give up, within a few years, all that we had believed from the beginning, before we had known white people and a Christian God. Many of us felt there was nothing in our religion to keep us from going to church and believing in the white man's god. That is, in fact, what many of our people did, and still do. They follow their own religion and go to some Christian church, and find good in both.

For some years, the Agents forbade us to hold any of our religious ceremonies—medicine dances, they called all our gatherings—and threatened to withhold our annuities and our rations if we took part in them. In return, our chiefs and Dog Soldiers, the strongest of our men's societies, sometimes tried to compel us to attend and take part in our old ceremonies. To do this, those of us who were trying to farm had to neglect our livestock and crops and so were in trouble with the Agency. We were wrong, whatever we did. But when Captain Lee came, he looked at things from both sides. He reasoned with us, though some of our Agents had said, and reported to Washington, that we could not reason. Captain Lee agreed to allow us to hold our annual medicine gathering, with his protection from interference, if we held it at a time when it would not interrupt our farming or our children's schooling. Things went better for us then, and we learned to be less fearful and sullen about our religion.

When I was a boy, a false religion sprang up that disturbed the Indians throughout the country for years. It was called the Ghost Dance, and began among the Paiute when one of them named Wovoka gave out word that he was the new Savior. He reported visions in which he learned that all dead Indians were to be resurrected and white people were to disappear from the earth and buffalo to return. New dances, done to singing without drums, were to be done for four nights every six weeks. All the people must dance wearing magpie feathers in their hair and carrying feather fans. As they danced, they might fall into a trance that brought long dead relatives and friends before them and showed them the Indian paradise that was to come. Rivers would flow in both directions, so that no one had to row upstream; berries and fruits would grow at a height where they could be picked without stooping or climbing; buffalo would be plenty always; the Indian dead would return; and there would be no more white people.

The new religion spread fast, first to the Shoshoni and then to one tribe after another, principally among the Plains Indians. Some of the Arapaho believed in this new Messiah; others were doubtful. In the winter of 1889 one of our Indian police, Black Coyote, and another Arapaho went to visit the new Messiah and decide for themselves whether his teachings were true or false. But the snows were so heavy in Wyoming that they could not reach him, and they came home undecided. Later the Kiowa chief Apiatan and the Arapaho Sitting Bull went to Wyoming, and came back to tell us that the new religion was false. The white men were not going to disappear; the buffalo would not return; our relatives and friends and heroes of old times would not come back to earth. We must go ahead on the new road we had taken.

Then, more than ever, we needed to carry out our old religious ceremonies, and more than ever the Government was determined to make us discontinue them. The old people were despondent and the young and better educated were confused. It was then that our chief Left Hand went to Agent Stouch to give him a better understanding of our plight. Left Hand, an orator and a leader in all things, made him see that our Man-Above and his God were the same, and that we differed only in the way we worshipped. "Our way," he said, "has come down to us through many generations, and is the only way we know. Among white people there are many ways of worshipping, and many kinds of belief about God. They are all tolerated, but our way is not tolerated. Our children go to school and learn your way and will worship as they are taught. But many of us are old, and can not change our ways. When we die, our way of worship will end. We are so sure that our God and your God are the same that we do not try to take our children away from you; we know your way is good, but we do not understand it. We want you to teach our children your way and let us follow our own. We invite you to come and visit our ceremonies, and to see that they are ancient and reverent and contain nothing harmful."

Major Stouch was deeply impressed with this speech, and wrote it in his report to Washington. It had changed his mind, he said, and he would not forbid our dances. We, on our side, agreed that we would not neglect our duties as farmers to hold them. The Major

even gave up trying to persuade our old men to cut their hair and
to dress as white men did. The best support he had in his work at
the Agency, he said, came from the old men who wore their hair in
long braids. Major Stouch recognized men of strong hearts when
he met them. He was our friend, as well as our Agent, and we made
great progress while he was there. But each year we built our medicine lodge again and held our ceremonies for the Sun Dance. Once
more we came together as one people with a good purpose, forget-
ting our quarrels and misfortunes and leaving, after the week was
ended, with hope and determination to live in peace and to be indus-
trious in the white man's way.

It is hard to explain these ceremonies to those who know nothing about them. They were more than a Sun Dance, for this was
only one part of the great undertaking. Even the priest in charge
did not know all of each day's ceremonies, but he knew what groups,
or societies, and what leaders were to carry out each particular part.
One man of the tribe made the vow, or the promise, that started the
preparations; he made it after a vision or much meditation, as a
great thank offering or to promote the health and welfare of himself or his family. His vow was to build the offerings lodge; he was
then called the Lodge-Maker for that year and was responsible, with
the priest, for setting the time and the place and for calling the
people together.

Everyone came for the encampment at the place where the
offerings lodge was to be built. People moved in from all directions,
winding over the prairies, visiting and singing as they came. Tipis
stood in a great circle, facing the morning sun and pointing their
poles toward the sky. This was a time to wear the finest clothes and
moccasins, to ride the best horses, and to bring all the food that
could be had for the feasting. For days the place looked like some
council grounds, and there was friendship and kindness in everyone's heart. Many people had special favors to hope for, such as the
healing of a sick child or the settling of a quarrel between husband
and wife. These people "wrapped the wheel" with an offering and
prayers for the favor they asked; others fasted and offered prayers
and danced, or took part in the special ceremonies of the society to

which they belonged. Even the children had special games, such as "Come This Way" and "Choosing Grandfathers," which they played during the encampment.

Those with the hardest part were the young men who vowed to do the Sun Dance. Purified and painted by their sponsors, or "grandfathers," fasting and without water, they must dance facing the center pole and blowing their whistles for long periods until all the ceremonies connected with the Sun Dance had been finished and they had greeted the sun on the final morning. There was no physical torture in the Arapaho dance, as many people believed and as was once true of the Sun Dance of some other tribes, but there was long fasting and need for great strength and endurance.

The offerings lodge was the center of these ceremonies. The center pole of this lodge was a large tree cut down and trimmed in the woods so that the branches made a fork at the top, and brought in with singing by the Dog Soldiers. It took a great deal of strength and skill to build the lodge, and those who did it each had their part to do in the same way that it had always been done. When it was finished it was a great round green shelter, with a center pole decorated with sacred things. Toward the close of the ceremonies, there were times when those who wished could make public gifts to the poor or as a reward to someone for a special kindness, of robes or ponies or other valuable things; and the chiefs made changes in the names of the men who had earned new names and inducted new chiefs who had been chosen, to replace any who had died or could no longer carry out their duties. In one of the last of the ceremonies, parents offered the outgrown clothes of their children, hanging them to the center lodge pole with prayers for the health and growth of the children. By the time the encampment broke up, there was happiness and good will among all the people, and hope for the year that lay ahead.

The sacred objects used in the ceremonies were wrapped and taken home by their keepers for the next gathering, but the offerings lodge, with all the offerings, was left as it stood, for Sun and Moon and Mother-Earth and the Four Old Men to dispose of in time. Long afterward, when we passed the place where a medicine lodge had stood, we remembered the vows and the blessing and the dancing and the feasting there, and our hearts were touched with the thought of how we had been lifted up and strengthened there.

It would be impossible for the Southern Arapaho to hold their full medicine-lodge ceremonies today. Most of the old men and women who knew the rites for the different societies are gone; the sacred objects are no longer kept renewed and purified; the societies no longer have enough members to carry out their duties. A much simpler ceremony, with some of the same meaning, has taken its place among many of the Arapaho and among other Indians as well. This is the ceremony of the Native American Church, the peyote ceremony.

Meetings of the Native American Church are held at night, usually Saturday night, in a tipi with a crescent-shaped altar where the peyote, or mescal, buttons are placed. Only men take part, wearing red blankets and carrying black feather fans. Those who take part eat peyote buttons and under its influence receive a vision, if they have prepared themselves by fasting and meditation. Singing, both by the priest in charge and by individuals, is one of the principal features of the ceremony. I have found it true that if some of the singers bring the feathers of the scissor-tailed fly-catcher with them, the singing takes on great power and the whole lodge is filled with a humming sound.

Here again, white people have misunderstood the Indians' worship and have tried to outlaw the Native American Church. They used to try to prove that peyote is a harmful narcotic and habit-forming. Yet soldiers who were members of this Church took part in both world wars and made fine records for themselves, with outstanding courage and endurance. Those who join in the ceremony do so to fulfill a vow, or for some improvement in their character or their minds or health. I have heard the experience of the peyote ceremony compared to that of communion in some of the Christian churches. When the service ends at sunrise, and the fast is broken with the water and the food that the women bring, those who have taken part face the day and the world before them with a new sense of beauty and hope and goodness in their hearts. Left Hand spoke the truth: There are many ways to God.

9

The End
of the Road

In 1891, our chiefs Left Hand, Row of Lodges, White-Eyed Antelope, Bull Thunder, Scabby Bull, Black Coyote, White Snake, White Buffalo, and Black Thunder made the last important agreement for the Southern Arapaho. Each member of our tribe was to be assigned a quarter-section of land for a farm, and all the land that was left was to be sold to the Government. Later the Cheyenne made the same sort of agreement, and in 1892 the surplus lands of the Southern Arapaho were opened to white settlement. This was the beginning of the end of our tribal life. Our schools were continued, and through the Agency we were still given assistance with our farm problems and were paid the money due to us from the sale of our land. As long as our Agents were such men as Captain Lee, Captain Woodson, and Major Stouch, our lives went on in much the same way as before. They helped us adjust to our new neighbors and protected our rights in our dealings with the newcomers.

But when Major Stouch retired, in 1906, things changed. Our new Agent, a man named Shell, showed nothing of the interest and sympathy with our problems that we had learned to count on, and seemed to be ready to do away with everything about our lives that was Indian. Soon he had combined the Government school for the Arapaho with that for the Cheyenne at Caddo Spring, and it was now called the Cheyenne-Arapaho School. Then the name Caddo Spring, that we had always known, was changed to Concho. I suppose the Agent hardly dared to call it Shell; so he named it for himself in Spanish.

The Agency grounds at Darlington are fenced and closed to the public now, and have been made a state game hatchery. Most of the old buildings are gone; the offices have been moved to Concho; the fine brick Mennonite Mission building is falling into decay and the ground around it is a wheat field. Fort Reno is no longer a fort, and the land that was a part of it is now used for grazing experiments. The parade ground is no longer trim and well kept, and the house that was once General Sheridan's headquarters has been moved away. There is nothing to be proud of there now.

No one knows quite how we lost this land where the Fort and the Agency stood or who agreed to give it up. We only know that hardly a landmark is left of what was once the center of our lives. The old Caddo Spring that once flowed in a clear stream and supplied water for the whole school is only a muddy puddle. If the ghost of Agent Shell came back, he would not be proud of this place that he named for himself. We never go to Darlington now, and when we go to El Reno or Concho we take the long way around to avoid it. But we still remember that it was once a place where we lived as Arapaho, and where good white people were friendly and kind and gave their lives to setting us on the new road of the white man.

A List of Paintings
by Carl Sweezy

Where no credit is given to an illustration, it is from the collection of the author.

No complete list of Carl Sweezy's paintings could be assembled. He was a professional in that he lived, especially during the latter years of his life, entirely by painting, but he was not a professional in any other sense. His way of selling was to put his work into a big portfolio tied up with rope and tramp around the town with it; he preferred to be paid in currency rather than by check because he had no bank account. He never made a list of his paintings or kept any record of where he sold them; yet somehow they have been widely dispersed. These, however, are a representative sample.

1. AN INDIAN PRIEST.

Courtesy of The Oklahoma Historical Society.

2. PIPE DANCE.

Courtesy of The Oklahoma Historical Society.

3. FIGHTING INDIANS.

4. A CHIEF.

Courtesy of The Oklahoma Historical Society.

5. THREE CHEYENNE WARRIORS.

Courtesy of Oscar B. Jacobson.

6. INSIDE A FAMILY TIPI.

7. AN INDIAN WARRIOR.

8. OKLAHOMA DANCERS.

Courtesy of Oscar B. Jacobson.

9. A WAR DANCE.

10. THE MEDICINE LODGE OF THE SUN DANCE.

11. A VILLAGE CHIEF WITH HIS DANCERS.

12. INDIANS ATTACKING BUFFALO HUNTERS.

13. INDIANS FIGHTING WHITE MEN.

Courtesy of The Oklahoma Historical Society.

14. SCRAPING A HIDE OUTSIDE A FAMILY TIPI.

15. INDIAN GAME FOR MEN AND BOYS—SNOW SNAKES.

16. INDIAN GAME FOR BOYS—WHIPPING TOPS.

17. INDIAN WAR.

18. PRAYER BEFORE ENTERING THE TIPI FOR A PEYOTE CEREMONY.

19. BUFFALO HUNTERS SKINNING A BUFFALO.

20. AN INDIAN WAR.

21. A WAR PARTY ATTACKING.

22. A PEYOTE CEREMONY.

Courtesy of Mrs. Gertrude Phillips.

DATE DUE

SEP 17			
MAR 3			
JUN 14			
FEB 10			
2-26-07			
GAYLORD			PRINTED IN U.S.A.